"*The Nation on No Map* draws on a rich genealogy of the Black Radical Tradition to challenge enduring conditions of white supremacist and capitalist domination. Recalling diverse lineages of Black anarchist political philosophy and praxis, William C. Anderson offers an urgent and incisive meditation for liberation—one that moves abolition beyond the state."

J. KĒHAULANI KAUANUI, author of *Paradoxes of Hawaiian Sovereignty: Land, Sex, and the Colonial Politics of State Nationalism*

"This is an extremely important contribution to the critical discourse on the nature of racism, elitism, misogyny, and other forms of hierarchy as primary manifestations of the nation-state. It includes a definitive explanation of the arrant dangers of charismatic leadership and individual celebrity worship that clouds our understanding of the real nature of authentic, valid social movement. Proceeding from the crystal clear and keenly observed accurate assumption that the nation-state must be dismantled in order to address the root cause of hierarchy in all of its ugly and violent forms, Anderson fills in a broad narrative full of human experience that helps us more fully comprehend the scope of our long-term human quest for a stateless and classless world devoid of all forms of social inequality."

MODIBO M. KADALIE PH.D., founding convener of the Autonomous Research Institute for Direct Democracy and Social Ecology and author of *Pan-African Social Ecology: Speeches, Conversations, and Essays*

WILLIAM C. ANDERSON

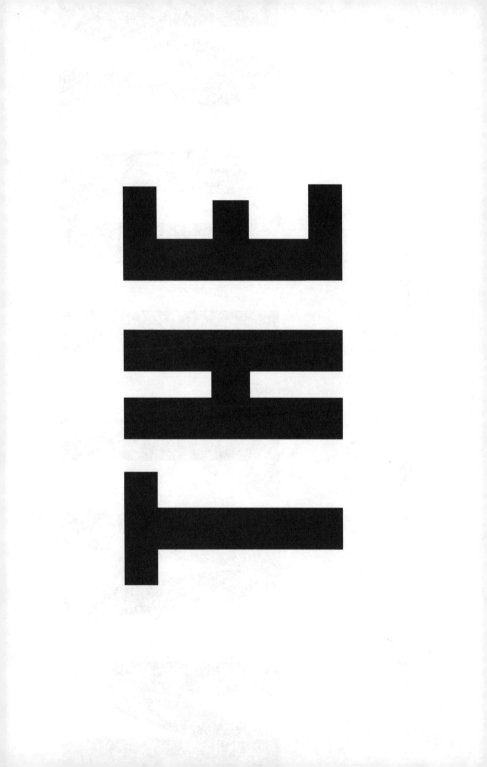

FOREWORD BY

SAIDIYA HARTMAN

AFTERWORD BY

LORENZO KOM'BOA ERVIN

BLACK ANARCHISM

AND

ABOLITION

AK PRESS

The Nation on No Map: Black Anarchism and Abolition
© 2021 William C. Anderson
This edition © AK Press (Chico/Edinburgh)

ISBN: 978-1-84935-434-9
E-ISBN: 978-1-84935-435-6
LCCN: 2021935969

AK Press
370 Ryan Ave. #100
Chico, CA 95973
www.akpress.org
akpress@akpress.org

AK Press
33 Tower St.
Edinburgh EH6 7BN
Scotland
www.akuk.com
akuk@akpress.org

The above addresses would be delighted to provide you
with the latest AK Press distribution catalog, which features
books, pamphlets, zines, and stylish apparel published and/or
distributed by AK Press. Alternatively, visit our websites
for the complete catalog, latest news, and secure ordering.

Cover and interior design by Crisis
Cover photograph: Joe Schwartz, *First Watts Festival—
After the Revolt*. Used with permission. Copyright Joe
Schwartz Photo Archive, www.joeschwartzphoto.com.
Interior photographs by William C. Anderson
Printed in Michigan on acid-free, recycled paper

CONTENTS

BLACK IN ANARCHY

"Anarchism" is an open word whose contours and meaning are shaped by the long struggle for Black liberation, by the centuries-long resistance to racial slavery, settler colonialism, capitalism, state violence, genocide, and anti-Blackness. "Anarchism" gathers and names the practices of mutual aid and the programs for survival that have sustained us in the face unimaginable violence. It unfolds with and as Black feminism and Indigenous struggle. It offers a blueprint for radical transformation, for the possibilities of existence beyond the world of scarcity and managed depletion, enclosure, and premature death. In *The Nation on No Map*, William C. Anderson elaborates the anarchism of Blackness, joining a cohort of radical thinkers devoted to dreaming and rehearsing how we might live otherwise in the present and break with the fatal terms of the given, the brutal imposed order of things. *The Nation on No Map* is a compact and expansive text that sketches the long history of Black struggle against racial slavery, U.S. apartheid, and the settler state and asks us to consider a vision of politics that no longer has the state as its object or horizon and eschews the calcified forms of politics as usual.

What shape might the radical imagination assume when the state is no longer the horizon of possibility or the telos of struggle?, asks

Anderson. The goal identified in these pages isn't to negate the state and preserve it on a higher level but to abolish it altogether. It is no longer a matter of trying to hold it accountable or appealing to it or striving to assume its power. We know better. There is too much history, too much blood to imagine that the apparatus of terror and violence might avail itself for our liberation or lend itself to uses other than policing and extraction, militarism and death.

Whither the state? In answering this question, Anderson reminds us that as Black folks our existence has been relegated outside the state and the social contract. For centuries, we have been abandoned by the state and not included within the embrace of person or citizen. We have lived inside the nation as eternal alien, as resource to be extracted, as property, as disposable population. We have been the tool and the implement of the settler and the master; we have existed as the matrix of capitalist accumulation and social reproduction; we have been the "not human" that enabled the ascendancy of Man. Our relation to the state has been defined primarily by violence. Our deaths, spectacular and uneventful, have provided the bedrock of the white republic.

This history explains how we have arrived at anarchism. Blackness is anarchic, writes Anderson, and Black people have been "engaged in anarchistic resistances since our very arrival in the Americas." All "without necessarily laying claim to 'anarchism' as a set of politics." The anarchism of Blackness emerges in the condition of statelessness experienced by Black people in the United States. Any pledge of allegiance is eclipsed by the charge of genocide and massacre, by stolen life and surplus death. "From the nonevent of emancipation to the afterlife of slavery, Black America has been required to consistently think outside of the state because the state has consistently been our oppressor." Statelessness, as Anderson explains, "is more than a lack of citizenship: it renders you nonexistent, a shadow. So why not embrace the darkness we're in, the darkness we are, and organize through it and with it?" Our struggles have challenged the authority and legitimacy of the state for as long as we have been in the Americas. With this in mind, Anderson asks that we imagine possibilities for radical transformation that no longer see the state as the arbiter of the possible or as the ultimate vehicle and realization of freedom.

What might be possible when our freedom dreams are not tethered to old forms? At the very least, the vision of what is and what might be are transformed, no longer yoked to the nation and capital. Other blueprints of the future emerge, Anderson suggests, when we are not stuck repeating the exhausted and failed strategies of the past. Invoking an oft-quoted line from Marx's *The Eighteenth Brumaire of Louis Bonaparte*, Anderson beseeches us to seek our poetry from the future rather than the past. Anarchism is one form of this poetry of the future.

"Anarchism" is an open and incomplete word, and in this resides its potential. It is to perceive possibilities not yet recognizable; it hints at what might be, at modes of living and relation that are unthinkable in the old frameworks. The goal isn't to establish a new orthodoxy or a new vanguard. Nor does Anderson attempt to integrate Black anarchism into the canon of European anarchist thought or to make it legible in its terms, or to convince disbelieving others of the significant lessons offered by the successive movements against state and empire and capital. Black anarchism is anarchism otherwise, and its goal is the reconstruction of everything. "Anarchism is just a name," Anderson writes. "Our revolution can be great no matter what we call it." The goal is transformation, to become "ungovernable masses to create a society where safety and abundance rule over us, not violence."

To be stateless, to be nowhere, is, for Anderson, to be situated in a transversal relation, a rhizomatic network of struggle everywhere. In sketching out the possibilities inherent in Black anarchism as a framework or moment for a global struggle against racial capitalism, settler colonialism, heteropatriarchy, and empire, anti-Blackness and statelessness provide the pivotal terms of his argument. Here there is no false opposition or impasse between the critique of anti-Blackness and a radical planetary vision. The task is to imagine change and work in the everyday for radical transformation, however it might be named: as riot, as insurrection, as rebellion, as intifada. So, what is necessary to achieve autonomy and liberation? A first step, Anderson notes, is to abandon the eternal verities and the old orthodoxies in their Marxist and Black nationalist forms, because they make the state the vessel of their ideality. The second is to embrace "poetry from the future" because only it can embrace the vision of another set of planetary arrangements, other possibilities of relation not predicated on hierarchy and centralized authority. The third is to create liberated or temporary autonomous zones, Black geographies of freedom that might be called the commune or the clearing.

Anarchism is the "inheritance" of the dispossessed, the legacy of slaves and fugitives, toilers and recalcitrant domestics, secret orders and fraternal organizations. It is the history that arrives with us— as those who exist outside the nation, as the stateless, as the dead, as property, as objects and tools, as sentient flesh. In meeting the heinous violence of the colony and the plantation, we have resisted, we have battled, we have fought to defeat our oppressors, we have struggled to live and to survive. In this protracted war, we have created networks of mutual aid, maroon communities, survival programs, and circles of care. We are Black in anarchy because of how we have lived and how we have died. We are Black in anarchy. *The Nation on No Map* illuminates the potentiality that resides there.

SAIDIYA HARTMAN

June 2021

ACKNOWLEDGMENTS

Thank you, whoever you are entertaining this work. I'm still learning how to read, and I'm still learning how to write. All of my writing is part of an ongoing process of growth and striving toward clarity and comprehension. I've only gotten this far through trial and error. As a writer and an activist, I get the great pleasure of going through this transformation in front of an audience. I do my best to understand the world around me and offer whatever I can. So, thanks for giving anything I do a chance.

Thank you to everyone who contributed to this project through input, edits, endorsement, or otherwise. Thank you to Lorenzo and Saidiya for contributing your words. I don't like attempting to name everyone because I would feel horrible if I left someone out. Thank you for being an inspiration and for your encouragement. Most importantly, thank you for your love. This book is not mine alone because the ideas in it are a combination of care, support, and compassion shown by people much better than me. It's written by the beauty of community and hopefully to the benefit of many. It's a wonderful thing, really, to see how chance meetings, personal histories, and full lives intersect to create new ideas.

So, for whomever it may be of use and whomever it may serve, here goes nothing!

I'd also like to send condolences to those mourning the countless lives lost due to the COVID-19 pandemic and state violence. I've seen several people that were dear to me pass away while writing this text, and many of us have suffered quite a bit. I hope we can all see better days together because we deserve so much more than this.

I have to thank my family for supporting me too. And to my sweet mother I just want to say I get it now, and thank you for telling me who I was before I could even see it. I do wish I could see you look at me and smirk like you used to, but I can still feel it. I would give anything to hug and kiss you and hold hands like we used to. I miss you every day, and I love you endlessly. Your spirit is with me.

INTRODUCTION

When I started writing this book, my politics were going through a dramatic shift. By the time I finished writing it, I was a new person. I learned what I was saying along the way after taking on too much at once for years. This is the journey many of us are always on politically. We make changes to what we believe, and we grow through learning. However, I must admit, sometimes I wish that I'd had people around to tell me or warn me about certain things I ultimately found out later. There are a lot of warnings in this text. Being in and among movements for years has given me some of the most rewarding and most traumatic experiences I can recall. I've been organizing, thinking, and writing since I was a teenager, and I'm still coming into myself, with these experiences guiding me every step of the way.

This project of mine, which I hope you'll give a chance, is not about defending some sect or protecting an institution. It's about some realizations I've had that I'd like to share. Various Black anarchisms and Black autonomous politics have been helpful to me as an aid in understanding some of the hurdles we face. They've helped me do this with more precision than other ideologies I've come across. This contribution outweighs many, but it does not eliminate that which came before it. Many of the things that I critique in this text are positions I held before I ever entertained anarchism. So much of what's being said here is from lived experience and not mere projected feelings. I only use this misnomer "anarchism" to outline certain principles that I don't compromise on, but it's really a placeholder. I don't run from it, as one of my teachers once said, but it's also something I don't run *to*. What does it mean to respect something or someone enough to be able to let go and work to transcend for the sake of liberation? Really, this writing is to try to help people in ways I feel I have been helped. And if help is hindered by the devices I use, I'll have to figure out what's next, won't I?

When Aimé Césaire wrote his famous letter resigning from the French Communist Party, he said something that stays with me:

> I believe I have said enough to make it clear that it is neither Marxism nor communism that I am renouncing, and that it is the usage some made of Marxism and communism that I condemn. That what I want is that Marxism and communism be placed in the service of black peoples, and not black peoples in the service of Marxism and communism. That the doctrine and the movement would be made to fit men, not men to fit the doctrine or the movement. And, to be clear, this is valid not only for communists. If I were Christian or Muslim, I would say the same thing. I would say that no doctrine is worthwhile unless rethought by us, rethought for us, converted to us. This would seem to go without saying.[1]

[1] Aimé Césaire, "Letter to Maurice Thorez," *Social Text* 28, no. 2 (June 2010): 149–50.

With that being said, we should avoid service to ideology and let all that we can gather from different ideas work in service to us. There is a collection of thoughts here across the spectrum of what we call "the left" and from radicals and thinking people of all sorts. I draw inspiration from many but seek no converts, nor do I want to testify to my own conversion. Any passion you see around my use of principles and concepts is the joy of thinking that we may be that much closer to helping ourselves attain true liberation. I want us to get there and not just talk about it or dream about it.

If I'm going to use paper and other resources to publish this text, I don't want to be wasteful. If you'll allow me, I'd like to tell you what my teachers have taught me and share how I've internalized it and what I think about the future. Everything I write and think is primarily influenced by the roar of a vacuum cleaner, calluses from dust mops, and the balance required to run a floor machine. It was the tough clarity given to me by the janitorial work that I have spent most of my life doing and by sitting with day laborers that informed my politics more than anything else in my life. I'm coming from a place where people don't have time to entertain nonsense, and I would very much like to keep that tradition alive with this text. I see no point in fueling fruitless debates while the world is in turmoil. However, there's great importance in lighting fires of urgency in anyone who should rightfully be fed up with sick, sorrowful societies.

I was raised by parents who informed me that I was not quite a citizen of the United States. This information influenced how I perceived all of the things I would experience throughout my life as a Black person in this country. By the time I was a teenager and I'd begun to do community organizing work, that's when I truly became immersed in questions of my placement in this society. Years of labor in different spaces led me to the immigrant rights movement after my home state of Alabama passed the Beason-Hammon Alabama Taxpayer and Citizen Protection Act, more commonly known as HB56. This anti-immigrant bill was part of a spate of similar legislation at the time that followed Arizona's infamous passage of SB1070. I became involved in my state because I understood the limits of citizenship as a Black American supposedly recognized as a citizen. I was not an immigrant, but I was the descendant of Black migrants who had moved all around the United States trying to escape the violence of racism and white supremacy.

I tried to explain as much in the immigrant rights movement to curious parties who were intrigued and fascinated by my involvement. Many of them saw my organizing and advocacy as charitable work or only a type of symbolic solidarity. I can even recall experiences where undocumented activists who were white demanded that I take more risks than them because I had "papers." They held citizenship over my head in a way that made me interrogate my position even more. It was by repeatedly explaining that being Black was not a safe haven that I first became interested in exploring anarchism. I'd seen what the state was capable of for years, but I gained a deeper perspective during the U.S. Immigration and Customs Enforcement (ICE) incursions against communities waged during the Obama administration. Late nights working alongside others on deportation cases, call campaigns, protests, civil disobedience, and fighting detention centers helped frame my thinking.

I saw the damage the idea of citizenship can cause and it gave me insights that I now write about at length. This coincided with a time in my life when I bounced around between ideas and sets of politics, again questioning identity and placement. I ultimately met Black anarchists Lorenzo Kom'boa Ervin and JoNina Ervin while I was co-leading a southern organizers' workshop. That chance meeting flipped everything I thought I knew on its head and reorganized my perspective with new language and political education to help me find my voice. Past frustrations I'd had in movement spaces and on the left were much clearer to me after I spent years reading and taking Black anarchism into consideration. That's what brings me to the current moment.

I'm not working to make Black anarchism appealing for academia, sanitize it for liberals, or make it a symbol voided of any real purpose. Anyone doing such things and mentioning my work in the process has nothing to do with me. I'm not here to be another loud, leftist, vanguardist man barking like I'm a general and everyone else is in my army, nor am I here to build a brand for myself. I *do* think there are things we need to be doing, but when I make such suggestions to readers, it is, I hope, in support of liberation, not any desire to be considered a leader.

Trying to meet all of our needs is more important than trying to have a successful career. These politics have helped people organize and understand the world that's crushing us. I'd like them to strengthen our efforts to get that weight off of our necks. At some points, I caught myself leaning into defending "anarchism" as an ideology—this was during the fascist state attacks on anarchists in 2020. I became fearful and paranoid because my politics have brought me more than my fair share of serious trouble before. We all consider ourselves experts on what everyone else is getting wrong, but I hope you'll understand that this book is pushing to break free from these cycles we get caught in. I wouldn't be bold enough to criticize much of what I do if this was not the point.

We should be wary of the coming waves of explanations of Black anarchism. These politics have gotten people killed, imprisoned, and tortured, and the least we can do is afford them their proper respect. Finishing this book helped me see the most complete picture of my politics I've ever had. *The Nation on No Map* comes in response to moments of crisis and widespread disaster unfurling around us at dangerous speeds. It is by no means a comprehensive or exhaustive introduction to Black anarchism, but it will trace and talk through my interpretations of the works that led me to the places I write from. I will mention people throughout this text who educated me about things I needed to know. Some I outgrew, don't agree with, and depart from at times. The point is, they taught me, and I'm speaking for myself through my writing.

Gwendolyn Brooks's poem about the Blackstone Rangers inspired the title of this book.

> Jeff. Gene. Geronimo. And Bop.
> They cancel, cure and curry.
> Hardly the dupes of the downtown thing
> the cold bonbon,
> the rhinestone thing. And hardly
> in a hurry.
> Hardly Belafonte, King,
> Black Jesus, Stokely, Malcolm X or Rap.
> Bungled trophies.
> Their country is a Nation on no map.[2]

Her poem, which touches on the organization of gangs that take on new names, new identity, and new shape, is something I've been

[2] Gwendolyn Brooks, "The Blackstone Rangers," in *Blacks* (Chicago: Third World Press, 1987), www.poetryfoundation.org/poems/43323/the-blackstone-rangers. Reprinted with consent of Brooks Permissions.

thinking about for many years now. Gangs and street organizations are an important part of the conversation I'm having in this text and in much of my work. These groups, often formed by people who have been forced to move and migrate to cities, help me think about Black America and our history. As I confront ideas about nation-building and/or trying to use or reform state power, I ultimately want to encourage others to take abolition and apply it to borders, nations, and states. I see the "nation on no map" as a group of people using skills others may struggle to recognize to develop new thinking, new language, and new societies. I envision a nation that doesn't need to be a nation and that doesn't need to be on a map, because it knows borders, states, and boundaries cannot accommodate the complexity of our struggles.

We've been in the mud for far too long, and, in the process of trying to come up out of it, some people have embraced some questionable methods. I am dedicated to liberation, and I'm committed to understanding it by whatever means I can. What's transpired throughout history is not merely something for me to criticize just because I can. The politics and ideas I've chosen to explore are a part of ongoing struggles that are very serious and too huge to be shrunken down to highlights. Having said this, I do hope people will study the revolutionary events that I draw from beyond what's referenced throughout this book.

I want to acknowledge that there are other Black radicals who already embrace much of the history, thought, and conclusions that I arrive at. It's not my intention to disrespect anyone who I don't know enough about yet, but I extend my love and solidarity to anyone reading who hopes to struggle together. I've shared commentary from thinkers who have an adversarial relationship with the past as well as those who are more open-minded to what it can represent. I think the truth is in a synthesis of both these positions. I also realize that I sometimes make my points using words from writers who arrived at very different conclusions from mine. What people like Lucy Parsons, W. E. B. Du Bois, Karl Marx, or C. L. R. James thought, of course, changed over time. I'd only like to point out that these transformations, whether I agree with where they led or not, represent the deeper core insight I feel we can see in the method of many Black anarchic and autonomous movements. We evolve and make use of what works for us, not as a means of repeatedly reinforcing our own doctrines but to create new revolutionary potential. We're on a journey, and it's best to travel with the willingness to think critically for the sake of growth.

This isn't about absolute truths or answers as much as it's about moving toward an active response to the problems that threaten our lives. Audre Lorde once warned Black men about sexism and patriarchy, writing, "It is not the destiny of Black america to repeat white america's mistakes. But we will, if we mistake the trappings of success in a sick society for the signs of a meaningful life."[3] What she wrote was also a blueprint for a free Black future. I think this applies to many of the things I try to think through in this book too. I come to you humbly as someone who has worked tirelessly and wants to share some of the things I've been journaling, reading, and thinking about. I hope it helps somebody.

Sincerely yours through struggle,

WILLIAM C. ANDERSON

---

[3] Audre Lorde, *I Am Your Sister: Collected and Unpublished Writings of Audre Lorde* (New York: Oxford University Press 2011), 47.

THE NATION

CHAPTER ONE

STATELESS BLACK

I'm from America but I'm not an American. —Malcolm X

I am stateless anyway. —Dionne Brand

In my language there is no word for citizen. —Keorapetse Kgositsile

We cannot accept what's happening around us. Those fed up with the way things are and resolved to fight for liberation already know as much. Yet, in order to achieve liberation, even those of us ready to fight have to get certain things out the way. There are structures, apparatuses, and institutions that need to feel the fire of our collective rage. But there are also boundaries drawn within us, within our ideas of who we are, that must be crossed. In order to achieve liberation, we will have to overcome the stories we've told ourselves about how wars like this can be won. If those stories and strategies were as effective in practice as we imagine, we would have already triumphed. This is what I want to explore: I believe we advance toward defeating empire, that global machinery of domination, only by surpassing many of the myths we tell ourselves about our pasts and our present. If we're not careful, these superstitions can aid the various forms of state violence we must work to end. The environment in which we fight for liberation is always changing, and we should be ready to adapt accordingly. This adaptation will happen at the expense of dangerous fictions like citizenships, states, and maps, and all the restrictions they entail. By understanding, using, and explicitly organizing around our positions as oppressed people, we can begin to undermine the unacceptable forms of governance forced onto our lives each day. We need to discuss the terrible predicament we're in, but time is of the essence.

I'm no expert, nor do I trust that term. I have simply gained an understanding of white supremacy by being Black and working class, by cleaning toilets as a janitor for the majority of my life growing up in the Deep South. My job and my class position, of course, have informed my politics. As a janitor, you learn intimately what's wrong with this society because you have to clean it up. You get to know society very well through its messes. How much someone despises you or fails to see you is apparent in what they leave behind for you to clean up. I repeatedly met capitalism and white supremacy with a mop in my hand and often wished it was a blade that I grasped instead. Many of us have felt this way. We feel the foot on our neck. We know the threats, terminations, and abuses, the stench of dismissal and hatred. Day after day we labor, dealing with the dirt of empire, which works to maintain its dominance through violence against oppressed people.

Black people's entire lives are shaped through an implicit understanding that we are not truly a part of the society we're born into. We are not really citizens, and our history tells us this without much ambiguity. As Dionne Brand notes, "Black experience in any modern city or town in the Americas is a haunting. One enters a room and history follows; one enters a room and history precedes. History is already seated in the chair in the empty room when one arrives."[1] History doesn't only haunt us Black people here in the United States, it does so across the Americas, throughout the West, and in the many different worlds where we live. We can join together in struggle to look at history honestly without fearing the new futures it may lead us to.

On my own journey, I have arrived at Black anarchism as a useful tool to help me think through these issues, but, although it holds a special place within my analysis, it does not hold me in place. I do not limit myself to traditionally "anarchist" concerns or just one form of Black anarchistic or autonomous politics, although all of these things and more help me process the work of abolishing unacceptable forces around us. When I speak of abolition—that is, the dismantling rather than mere reforming of the institutions that maintain capitalism, white supremacy, and other oppressions—I am not focused on one aspect of a despicable situation as much as I am

[1] Dionne Brand, *A Map to the Door of No Return: Notes to Belonging* (Toronto: Vintage Canada, 2001), 24.

questioning the situation as a whole. The United States does not *have* problems, the United States *is* the problem. The same goes for other states that have built themselves up off of slavery, genocide, conquest, and colonialism—which is far too many of them. While I happen to live within U.S. borders, much of what needs to be understood about our fight applies around the world, but my focus here is primarily on the U.S. empire.

The lie that we live in a great, equitable democracy damages countless people who are forced to carry the weight of this myth. Believing that this is the best version of a society, as it claims to be, transforms our hardships, our poverty, and unhappiness into something that's our own fault. This is a deadly lie. How this country was created and how it continues to function will destroy us all if we don't expand the work to abolish it as soon as possible. It's not just the police, the Supreme Court, the Senate, or the military: the entirety of this fatal project must be brought to an end.

There are many different approaches we can take. As Lorraine Hansberry once said, "I think . . . that Negroes must concern themselves with every single means of struggle: legal, illegal, passive, active, violent and nonviolent. That they must harass, debate, petition, give money to court struggles, sit-in, lie-down, strike, boycott, sing hymns, pray on steps—and shoot from their windows."[2] These

---

[2] Lorraine Hansberry, *To Be Young, Gifted and Black: Lorraine Hansberry in Her Own Words*, adapted by Robert Nemiroff (Saddle River, NJ: Prentice-Hall,

efforts must necessarily work to delegitimize the state's monopoly on violence.

As previously stated, a Black anarchist lens helped develop the language I use to describe our condition in this country. In 2017, I coauthored an article with Zoé Samudzi, "The Anarchism of Blackness."[3] This was the term we used to describe the statelessness experienced by Black people in the United States. Our position was that Black people are *residents in* but not *citizens of* the United States, a condition that has the potential to prime Black people for an insurrectionary set of politics should they choose to embrace it this way. Our goal, and mine here, was to recognize and encourage separation from all positive identification with the United States. Through collective detachment, more people can see less reason to negotiate with oppression.

We must ask ourselves: are our politics as unrelenting as the resolve of the deadly oppressive forces we're up against? Those who seek our demise are not slowing down or easing up. In fact, it often feels like things are getting worse. People who insist on compromising with the forces that are determined to exterminate us are only attempting to rearrange the terms of a perpetual crisis. This is the

---

1969), 213–14. The quote is taken from a letter Hansberry wrote to white southerner Kenneth Merryman on April 27, 1962.

[3] William C. Anderson and Zoé Samudzi, "The Anarchism of Blackness," *ROAR Magazine* 5 (Spring 2017): 70–81.

liberal language of reform. As we deteriorate, advocates of an incremental approach to deadly situations put lives at risk whether they mean to or not. They insist that the intolerable be tolerated for some unspecified but never-ending period of time. Over and over, problems too big to be reformed away are given new chances to be rewired—and we're somehow shocked every time things remain the same. The absurdity here is one of telling someone in chains that the problem is only that their shackles are too tight or too short. The real problem is the existence the chains themselves. So, while we wait ad infinitum for reforms to chip away at what's enchaining us, more and more lives are lost, just to give the reformers the opportunity to specify again what is not working. This is unequivocally true across the board for reforms in the areas of "criminal justice," economics, and civil rights. Black people know these reform struggles all too well.

This is why at the very least our politics should be as unflinching and all-encompassing as what we're fighting. Honestly, they must go even further. For that to happen, we must free ourselves of the strangleholds of the problems that come with reform, citizenship, and patriotism. These problems are sustained, in part, by how we interpret the historical struggles that precede us.

The civil rights movement is selectively remembered in popular and state-sponsored retellings of history, reducing a complex phenomenon to favored leaders, organizations, and actions. The dis-

torted focus on reformist efforts creates a battle within history itself. In order to move forward, we are forced to confront misleading versions of what transpired and to what extent. When movement history is reduced to something only marked by progressive legislation and political reforms that adjust how white supremacist institutions function, it happens at the expense of that history's more confrontational and radical aspects. Thankfully, we have radical retellings and testimonies to counter this, but even some of these are underappreciated. A founder of contemporary Black anarchism, Lorenzo Kom'boa Ervin, repeatedly critiques reformism and addresses this aspect of the movement directly, relating it to our situation today.

At this juncture the movement can go into the direction of revolutionary social change, or limit itself to winning reforms and democratic rights within the structure of Capitalism. The potential is there for either. In fact, the weakness of the 1960s civil rights movement was that it allied itself with the liberals in the Democratic Party and settled for civil rights protective legislation, instead of pushing for social revolution. This self-policing by the leaders of the movement is an abject lesson about why the new movement has to be self-activated and not dependent on personalities and politicians.[4]

[4] Lorenzo Kom'boa Ervin, *Anarchism and the Black Revolution.* Published in 1993, this work has been reprinted many times. It is available at theanarchist library.org/library/lorenzo-kom-boa-ervin-anarchism-and-the-black-revolution.

We have not been able to achieve liberation through reformist inclusion or greater participation in the ruling system itself. No matter how much we achieve, accumulate, or excel at playing the game, we're always capable of being caged, repressed, brutalized, or killed because we're Black. We cannot vote this away. Black people have only been supposedly allowed to vote for a short time, and our only choices are two parties serving the interests of a ruling class. The system that we're used to will neutralize any real threats that advocate actual change. Voter suppression and deception are built into elections as we know them, especially at the national level where the Electoral College determines outcomes. The "tools" we are offered can build nothing new. Their efficacy is an illusion. It has been a constant struggle to maintain even the largely symbolic right of Black people to vote. Voter ID laws, background checks, gerrymandering, and modern-day poll taxes are just some of the methods levied against us. They're extensions of what has happened to us as Black people since our earliest efforts to gain the right to vote. They exist because the voting system was not meant or designed for us, so reforms and amendments to grant us access are always under threat.

Consider the 2013 Supreme Court case *Shelby County v. Holder*.[5] This 5–4 ruling struck down a key part of the Voting Rights Act of

---

[5] *Shelby County v. Holder*, 570 U.S. 529 (2013).

1965, which had been heralded as one of the great victories linked to the efforts of the civil rights movement. The majority opinion of the court, written by Chief Justice John Roberts, stated, "Nearly 50 years later, things have changed dramatically." With regard to Black people being systematically oppressed, of course, not nearly enough had changed in that nearly half-century. This was a victory for right-wing politicians and white supremacists across the country. However, it was a lesson for those of us whom the Voting Rights Act was supposed to protect. Everything that we claim as an accomplishment through machinery that our oppressors control can ultimately be undone. Do we work continuously, trying to make this machinery favor us through reformism, or do we abandon the idea altogether that this machinery is redeemable? This is an abolitionist question, and it applies to much more than voting, but in order to even begin to ask or answer questions like this we must overcome false history.

We have ancestors who did indeed fight and die for our right to cast votes. We also have ancestors who died for much more. Here again, historical struggles get forced into a single cohesive narrative, where radical efforts and aberrations can be lost. There were ancestors who did not just want a right to vote or participate in the U.S. project. Surely there were those who wanted the unjust, cruel governance lording over them to be done away with in its entirety. Yet we won't often or easily find accounts of them or their views mentioned in liberal retellings of Black history. But it is good for us to know that some of the people we come from wanted us to forsake unrealistic means of achieving liberation altogether, and they pointed us toward something much better. Voting may have had its uses at times, but the emphasis put on it as the primary way to make change by the liberal establishment is misleading, to say the least.

In a lecture given at the end of the nineteenth century, Lucy Parsons, a radical Black anarchist organizer who had been born into slavery, lamented the ineffectiveness of voting. "Anarchists know that a long period of education must precede any great fundamental change in society, hence they do not believe in vote-begging, nor political campaigns, but rather in the development of self-thinking individuals. We look away from government for relief, because we know that force (legalized) invades the personal liberty of man, seizes upon the natural elements and intervenes between man and natural laws; from this exercise of force through governments flows nearly all the misery, poverty, crime and confusion existing in society."[6]

In a 1905 piece in *The Liberator*, she famously raised an undying point, "Of all the modern delusions, the ballot has certainly been

---

[6] Lucy Parsons, "The Principles of Anarchism," in *Freedom, Equality and Solidarity—Writings and Speeches, 1878–1937* (Chicago: Charles H. Kerr, 2004), 31.

A student sees King

the greatest. Yet most of the people believe in it."[7] She warned voters and reformists, pointing out that even "winning" at the ballot box meant nothing:

> With thousands of laws being enacted and hundreds of corruptionists playing their tricks, what becomes of the voter's victory at the polls? What becomes of his reforming all things by the use of the ballot? So long as he is willing to submit to a bad law until it is repealed, what better leverage do rogues want on humanity? The fact is money and not votes is what rules the people. And the capitalists no longer care to buy the voters, they simply buy the "servants" after they have been elected to "serve." The idea that the poor man's vote amounts to anything is the veriest delusion. The ballot is only the paper veil that hides the tricks.[8]

Over a century after Parsons said this, many are still trying to convince us that voting offers solutions—solutions we know it cannot provide. Keep in mind that Lucy Parsons, a Black woman criticizing reformism and voting, did not have the right to vote at the time she wrote this in 1905. Her story, alongside those of others who similarly criticized voting, like W. E. B. Du Bois, disturbs the tale that all of our ancestors died for the right to vote. Du Bois echoed

[7] Lucy Parsons, "The Ballot Humbug," in ibid., 95.

[8] Ibid., 97.

Parsons decades later in 1956, writing in a piece titled "I Won't Vote," "There is but one evil party with two names, and it will be elected despite all I can do or say."[9]

Presenting the Black liberation struggle as a singular struggle with one line of thinking is a state project in and of itself. These modified versions of history attempt to give Black people a stake in the violence, excess, and rot of the United States, making it into something that we have all fought to lay claim to. Our struggles become, in this false narrative, a long march to be a part of the United States. We become homogenous in museums, textbooks, and state-sponsored institutions that are assigned the task of retelling our story. In the process, what is recalled as Black history becomes *everyone's* story, something everyone owns as a source of nationalist pride. Although it has been Black people who have fought against violence and brutality, our pain becomes a collective, national pain. Our wounds have not yet healed, but we're still being disenfranchised, now by the fiction of a past that has changed into a supposedly better present.

I describe this in a previous essay:

Popular versions of civil rights history portray harm, death, and hardship as necessary growing pains that helped develop the character of the US empire. Therefore, the egregious suffering that Black people

[9] W. E. B. Du Bois, "I Won't Vote," *The Nation*, October 20, 1956.

endured and still face today is made into a medallion representing this country's supposed collective freedom. According to this reasoning, we have to be brutalized to have a shot at being recognized as human; this particular victimization qualifies us to be a part of this country, which also regularly criticizes Black people for being victims. Black people are martyrs, willingly or not, for the nation's betterment.[10]

It benefits the state and our oppressors for us to remain invested in the story of reform rather than abolition, despite the fact that many of the promises of citizenship remain unattainable for us. Black liberals who adopt this incremental approach become extremely focused on assimilation, integration, and joining the so-called middle class. Meanwhile, poor and working-class people are reduced to talking points to achieve the goals of "reforms" that do little to change their situation. Fighting in the courts and in the hallways of the institutions that continue to do us harm is overemphasized as the sole way to bring about better conditions. It's worth examining one of the most famous court cases in U.S. history as a testament to our noncitizen condition.

Dred Scott and Harriet Robinson Scott, a Black couple who'd been enslaved, fought for their freedom in the courts. Their case is

[10] William C. Anderson, "Giving Up Patriotism and Integration Myths for MLK Day," *Truthout*, January 15, 2018, https://truthout.org/articles/giving-up-patriotism-and-integration-myths-for-mlk-day.

remembered as one of the most important leading up to the U.S. Civil War because of what it said about Black people and our position in this society. The Scotts' lawsuit was based on the fact that they'd spent time in the free state of Illinois and in Wisconsin Territory (which had also outlawed slavery) with the man who was considered their owner. They argued that having resided in so-called "free" areas entitled them to freedom. In 1857, the Supreme Court denied their claims in a 7–2 ruling that inflamed the country further. The court explained, "The words 'people of the United States' and 'citizens' are synonymous terms," and it went on to say, when it came to Black people, "We think they are not, and that they are not included, and were not intended to be included, under the word 'citizens' in the Constitution, and can therefore claim none of the rights and privileges which that instrument provides for and secures to citizens of the United States."[11]

Since the Scotts' case made it to the Supreme Court, it sent a message to a country experiencing increasing conflict around the question of slavery. Over 150 years later, Black people still represent a direct conflict with the concept of citizenship, by simply existing. These conflicts are not limited to the United States. For example, in Mexico it wasn't until 2015 that the country conducted a survey that finally recognized Afro-Mexicans. This recognition of African-

[11] U.S. Supreme Court, *The Case of Dred Scott in the United States Supreme Court* (New York: H. Greeley, 1860), www.loc.gov/item/10034357.

descended or Black Mexicans was celebrated, but the delay of this acknowledgement is telling. It underlines the mistreatment, disregard, and racism experienced by Black people throughout South and Central America where slave ships dropped off a large portion of those captured for enslavement in the Americas. In Portugal, Afro-Portuguese people have been denied citizenship even if they were born in the country. "It is an issue that, for reasons that are at the same time historical, socioeconomic and political, predominantly affects Portugal's black, Afro-descendent communities, who originate mostly in the African former colonies of Cape Verde, Angola, Guinea-Bissau, Sao Tome and Principe, and Mozambique."[12]

In England, the state was exposed by the Windrush scandal in 2018. The "Windrush generation" was named for the ship that brought some of the first immigrants from the Caribbean to England after World War II in order to fill labor shortages. These British subjects had the right to relocate, but many of these Black people were not provided with immigration papers, and landing cards that did exist were destroyed by the government in 2010. Decades after they had arrived, in a series of actions that highlight the perpetual contradiction between Black people and citizenship, this lack of "proper documentation" allowed them to be subjected to harass-

[12] Ana Naomi de Sousa, "The Portuguese Denied Citizenship in Their Own Country," *Al Jazeera*, March 23, 2017, www.aljazeera.com/indepth/features/2017/03/portuguese-denied-citizenship-country-170302084810644.html.

ment and deportation. They were denied benefits, health care, bank accounts, and driver's licenses; they lost jobs and homes and had their passports confiscated. How they were treated as outsiders in the country they called home shows exactly how the government views them.[13]

It was recognizing the sort of statelessness we experience that led to an essential moment in the development of Black anarchism. Before Lorenzo Kom'boa Ervin was an anarchist, he was a Maoist whose activism eventually led to him being accused of gunrunning and threatening to bomb a Klan-sympathizing judge. Lorenzo fled to Atlanta and later hijacked a plane to Cuba. He was met with hostility from the Cuban authorities, who imprisoned him amid tensions between the Cuban government and other Black radicals who'd fled there. Here we're forced to confront contradictions and history again. Ervin disturbs the popular narrative that situates Cuba as a safe haven where Black people can flee to be free from oppression. His story can be placed alongside others, like the Black revolutionary Robert F. Williams who also fled to Cuba and was met with hostility from the Cuban authorities, who he said ultimately began to "sabotage" his liberation work.[14] Williams said,

[13] "Windrush Generation: Who Are They and Why are They Facing Problems?," *BBC News*, April 18, 2018, www.bbc.com/news/uk-43782241.

[14] *Let It Burn: The Coming Destruction of the USA?*, directed by Robert Carl Cohen (Los Angeles: Radical Films, 2006).

"As far as the Black man is concerned, there's no such thing as a neutral country in the world."[15]

Ervin learned this in a way similar to many other Black radicals who fled from country to country, from state to state. He was deported from Cuba to Czechoslovakia, where he faced more hostility before he fled to what was then East Germany, where he was captured and tortured by U.S. authorities. He found no asylum in states that were at odds with the United States. He was eventually sent to a federal detention center in New York City, where his life took a dramatic turn during his chance encounter with a jailhouse lawyer and Black radical educator named Martin Sostre. It was Martin, a famous political prisoner at the time, who would introduce Lorenzo to anarchism, which led to his writing his foundational text, *Anarchism and the Black Revolution*. His political consciousness led him to flee just as it led him to confront the contradictions he experienced living under state socialism. He ended up back where he started and decided to begin anew by shedding the limitations of orthodoxy. In doing so, he changed his future and that of many others.

These are just a few examples of many. We can't truly say that anywhere in this world is for us without being proven wrong again and again. Perhaps part of the problem is that nations and states have long treated this planet and its resources as always being *for* some-

15 Ibid.

one. The oppressive state structure we attempt to survive under grants extractive rights based on the idea of citizenship. Since the very beginning of the United States, the right to land and natural resources and the right to commit acts of violence against people— Indigenous, Black, or otherwise—have been closely linked to citizenship. To be a citizen has meant to be white and, like whiteness, citizenship itself is an invention that is of no good use to us here. It has done much more harm than good. Anything that affords some people more rights than others based on borders, race, or class should be abolished. It has no redeeming quality for Black people, and fighting to be recognized by or within it means seeking to be embraced by something that has our rejection, if not extermination, built into its very definition. The contours of this situation are explicitly understood by undocumented people, migrants, refugees, and many others. Just as much is understood doubly so by Black people who try to survive under these categories, although it can be just as clear to Black people who don't have these immigration statuses, given the precariousness of our circumstances throughout the history of this country.

Though those of us descended from enslaved Africans were born here and have roots in the United States, that guarantees very little. The rights supposedly enshrined in state documents don't change the facts of our day-to-day reality. Neither birth certificates nor the U.S. Constitution grant us anything that can't be stripped away

Littered "stolen votes" from a performance in Atlanta

from us at any moment. This is just one reason the police are able to murder us regularly without any consequences. It's also why the first Black president had to repeatedly defend his citizenship and reconfirm his legal status. It's why we can have our voting rights and protections violated and why we've always been told to "go back to Africa" when we complain about injustices. This monster before us is insidious, and those of us interested in liberation have to pronounce this through historical truth-telling and political education to make any real, revolutionary progress.

Nothing that I'm writing here is new. Black radicals, thinkers, and activists of all ideological affiliations have long been doing the work I'm trying to attend to here. The terms, conditions, and details we face today may be different, but the work has been going on for quite some time. Many Black radicals have already said, in ways both explicit and implicit, that we are stateless within the borders of the empire, states, and nations that dismiss us.

In the essay "The Anarchism of Blackness," Zoé Samudzi and I attempted to explain how our problems as Black people will not be solved by liberalism or its party politics. "Due to this extra-state location, Blackness is, in so many ways, anarchistic. African-Americans, as an ethnosocial identity [composed] of descendants from enslaved Africans, have innovated new cultures and social organizations much like anarchism would require us to do outside of state structures. Black radical formations are themselves fundamentally antifascist despite functioning outside of 'conventional' Antifa spaces, and Black people have engaged in anarchistic resistances since our very arrival in the Americas."[16]

Being Black regularly places us in a position of opposition to the state whether we choose to accept that placement or not. Elsewhere, Zoé and I put it this way: "Blackness is the antistate just as the state is anti-Black."[17] That is not to say Black people are inherently radical or that Black people don't work in service to the state. It helps us understand that many aspects of Black history seen as "progress" could be more accurately described as concessions and temporary offerings from our oppressors that have very little to do with our happiness or safety. What has changed has done so through struggle, but the issues we battle with are enshrined in the core of the state's skeleton. Our history is full of countless occasions in which Black people, as communities and individuals, are doing our best to survive, only to be met with the most heinous violence imaginable. It has required us to react and survive in anarchistic ways without necessarily laying claim to "anarchism" as a set of politics.

So, we're Black in anarchy because of how we're treated and positioned in society based on our being Black. What I'm unpacking here is related to what writer and educator Saidiya Hartman de-

[16] Anderson and Samudzi, "The Anarchism of Blackness," 77.

[17] Zoé Samudzi and William C. Anderson, *As Black as Resistance: Finding the Conditions for Liberation* (Chico, CA: AK Press, 2018), 95.

scribes as "waywardness," although neither waywardness nor the anarchism of Blackness is reducible to anarchism as an ideology or doctrine. Hartman poetically defines it this way: "Waywardness is an ongoing exploration of *what might be*; it is an improvisation with the terms of social existence, when the terms have already been dictated, when there is little room to breathe, when you have already been sentenced to a life of servitude, when the house of bondage looms in whatever direction you move. It is the untiring practice of trying to live when you were never meant to survive."[18]

Black people seeking liberation present great potential to counter the system because we exist directly in contradiction to the system. Its loss can be our gain. We're forced to survive, no matter where we try to escape in terms of class, history, or geographic location. We cannot escape our skin. This situation has been dropped on our heads, and, because we live in it, with it, and against it, our understanding of freedom is fragmented because we have never completely experienced it. The Black freedom struggle is a struggle because the idea of a free Black population is not acceptable to a white supremacist state. Achieving Black liberation means a complete rejection of white supremacist society in its entirety.

Part of what obstructs us here is that "freedom" is too often de-

---

[18] Saidiya Hartman, *Wayward Lives, Beautiful Experiments: Intimate Histories of Social Upheaval* (New York: W. W. Norton, 2019), 227.

fined according to the oppressive standards of those who keep us from it. The holiday of Juneteenth reminds us of this every year. When Union general Gordon Granger and his troops arrived in Galveston, Texas, months after Confederate general Robert E. Lee surrendered in Virginia, they came to enforce the Emancipation Proclamation. The news arrived late, and for some it didn't arrive at all. Abraham Lincoln issued the Emancipation Proclamation on January 1, 1863, but the celebration in Galveston didn't take place until June 19, 1865. So, months after the war had ended and years after the initial order, Black people were able to celebrate what would amount to a reform of sorts. One hideous institution led to another hideous institution.

Saidiya Hartman's description of "the nonevent of emancipation" regarding the continuance of the plantation system and the "refiguration of subjection" is important for many reasons, but it's especially useful to us in rejecting the idea that we're actually free.[19] Emancipation was a nonevent because enslavement continued despite an announcement that it was ending. It was transformed into sharecropping and convict leasing and eventually found new life in the prison system. As Du Bois stated in *Black Reconstruction*, "The slave went free; stood a brief moment in the sun; then moved back

[19] Saidiya Hartman, *Scenes of Subjection: Terror, Slavery, and Self-Making in Nineteenth-Century America* (New York: Oxford University Press, 1997), 116.

again toward slavery."[20] Hartman's concept of "the afterlife of slavery," which she describes as "skewed life chances, limited access to health and education, premature death, incarceration, and impoverishment," is relevant here as well.[21] From the nonevent of emancipation to the afterlife of slavery, Black America has been required to consistently think outside of the state because the state has consistently been our oppressor. The truth of our history tells us that freedom has always been more of a concept than a reality. Using the word "freedom" at all to describe Black people's status is dubious and largely inaccurate. For this reason, celebrations like Juneteenth commemorations are complicated cultural events. We must be able to distinguish between relative improvements and actually achieving liberation. This isn't a dismissal of any past victories. Instead, it's an acknowledgement of the work that needs to be done, given the ongoing disaster we're living in that is not being reformed away.

The Black Panther Party for Self Defense is an important piece of Black history that draws the connections between the limitations of Black citizenship and revolution as opposed to reform. The party has been romanticized but is less likely to be mainstreamed as a

[20] W. E. B. Du Bois, *Black Reconstruction in America* (New York: Free Press, 1998), 30.

[21] Saidiya Hartman, *Lose Your Mother: A Journey Along the Atlantic Slave Route* (New York: Farrar, Straus and Giroux, 2008), 6.

model for action like the civil rights movement. These days, many activists mimic the Panther style and aesthetic while engaging a more popular electoral strategy that centers working within the state and its systems. The Panthers' radical legacy is something to be cosplayed, while ignoring the actual elements that made the organization most effective. Though the party was not without its problems, what the Black Panthers accomplished needs to be understood today in order to decenter reformism in favor of abolition.

Decades after the Black Panther Party was at its height, the relevance of some programs remains especially important. Certainly one of the organization's most obvious achievements was what we know today as their survival programs. The Panthers established community service programs that were there to address the shortcomings and neglect of institutions that were not living up to their supposed purposes. These programs grew out of an ideological position that Black Panther leader Huey P. Newton called "intercommunalism." Newton's idea of intercommunalism, while far-reaching—indeed global—in scope, involved thinking outside the logic of the states and governments that neglected (or worsened the conditions of) oppressed communities, while at the same time stepping up to meet the basic needs left unattended by that disregard.

In practice, countering neglect was very gendered labor. The work and the material efforts that it took to implement these programs fell heavily on the Black women who took on organizing efforts both for the party's sake and for their households. In her

For the "Little Rock Nine"

essay, "Framing the Panther: Assata Shakur and Black Female Agency," Joy James notes: "Hundreds of women, including Shakur before she was forced underground, served in the Black Panther Party's rank and file, implementing the medical, housing, clothing, free breakfast, and education programs. Female Panthers displayed an agency that (re)shaped American politics, although their stories recede in popular culture before the narratives of elites or icons."[22] Surely a lot can be learned from the words Huey wrote and spoke, but the core of historical truth and the substance of what we need to learn about survival programs is in the work these Black women carried out.

Since the state never has lived up to its rhetoric and never will, Black people have *always* had to implement survival programs, which shows quite clearly that we are not supposed to reap even the standard benefits of citizenship. This was happening long before the Black Panthers created health care clinics, free breakfast programs, or ambulance services. However, the ideological line drawn by the Panthers here is important. They were not just meeting needs through charity or philanthropy, they were politicizing people and threatening the state itself by doing so.

The intentional neglect perpetuated by the state requires a re-

[22] Joy James, "Framing the Panther: Assata Shakur and Black Female Agency," in *Want to Start a Revolution? Radical Women in the Black Freedom Struggle*, edited by Dayo F. Gore, Jeanne Theoharis, and Komozi Woodard (New York: NYU Press, 2009), 140.

sponse, and that response must be part of a revolutionary process. In the moments when we are not engaged in an explicitly revolutionary uprising, the process leading up to that point is of the utmost importance. What we do to address the great lack of resources Black people face is crucial for the process of building a mass movement. People often won't, and shouldn't, join a movement that's not truly meeting their needs. That's what exploitation and manipulation look like. A thorough preparation for revolt requires the survival of the people who are supposed to be doing the revolting.

Furthermore, the programs we need shouldn't simply be reacting to crises. We know and can identify what many of our problems are. The work of organizing isn't simply waiting and trying to counter whatever oppressive forces do to us; it is building and strengthening our very existence.

Newton said that survival programs were not the answer to the "whole problem of oppression" but positioned them as something "for the people," saying that "only the people make revolutions."[23] In his speech at Boston College, he gave an analogy about what a survival program represented, saying, "It is a program that works very much like the first aid kit that is used when a plane falls and you find yourself in the middle of the sea on a rubber raft. You need a few things to last until you can get to the shore, until you can get

[23] Huey P. Newton, "Speech Delivered at Boston College: November 18, 1970," in *To Die for the People: The Writings of Huey P. Newton*, edited by Toni Morrison (New York: Vintage, 1972), 21.

to that oasis where you can be happy and healthy. If you do not have the things necessary to get you to that shore, then you will probably not exist."[24] The everyday reality of Black life requires something comparable but through a mass effort aimed at our collective survival. This is where many elements of Black anarchism and our struggle against the state become increasingly relevant. Lorenzo Kom'boa Ervin explains:

> The Black Panther Party first put forward the concept of intercommunalism in the 1960s and, although slightly different, it is very much a libertarian concept at its core. (This used to be called "Pan Africanism," but included mainly "revolutionary" governments and colonial or independence movements as allies). Because of the legacy of slavery and continuing economic neocolonialism, which has dispersed Blacks to every continent, it is feasible to speak of Black international revolutionary solidarity.
>
> Here is how Anarchists see the world: the world is presently organized into competing nation-states, which through the Capitalist Western nations have been responsible for most of the world's famine, imperialism and exploitation of the non-white peoples of the earth. In fact, all states are instruments of oppression.[25]

[24] Ibid.

[25] Ervin, *Anarchism and the Black Revolution.*

Newton acknowledged the conflicts and contradictions around statehood and nation building. The Panthers adopted a push for revolutionary intercommunalism. Newton said this strategy grew out of a recognition that, under imperialism, the world was no longer run by nations but by ruling elites who formed alliances that created the conditions of "reactionary intercommunalism." Those who bore the brunt of empire also comprised scattered global communities that needed their own form of "revolutionary intercommunalism" in order to fight back. Sadly, these words still ring true today, and the astronomical wealth of the ruling class, as well as its transnational quality, has only increased. The strategic concept of survival programs is still relevant, because those who control wealth are only taking more and more from our communities. The climate crisis is growing worse by the day, as is the fascistic reach of governance.

Those of us inside U.S. borders who are attempting to take a stand against oppression are currently without a powerful oppositional movement. The Democratic and the Republican Parties both serve as administrators for the same ruling class interests, capitalism, and empire. Without a functioning, organized mass movement to truly counter the increasingly violent institutionalized intolerance we face, we must start simply by maintaining our survival to sustain ourselves for the long fight ahead. The everyday scourges of racism, sexism, ableism, homophobia, transphobia, and a wide array of other forms of discrimination are being amplified by the miserable

View from the NMAAHC

times we must survive through. Globally, fascism is growing, and sometimes it can seem hopeless to stand against it. Even here, Black tactics and traditions of survival are key. The Black experience of fascism in the United States is distinct in its violence and often provides a clear picture of what needs to be done. We know what fascism is because it's there on the faces of our killers.

Surviving this all is one thing, but moving beyond that to claim our right to be liberated and safe is another.

Our collective embrace of survival programs is one way of confronting history in order to create a better present and future. Statelessness is more than a lack of citizenship: it renders you nonexistent, a shadow. So why not embrace the darkness we're in, the darkness we are, and organize through it and with it? *Use* the conditions that the state has placed on us to inform our most radical incursions, rather than asking the state to change, when we should know by now that it certainly won't. The state is not for us. This sort of work, making do and building from exactly where we are has always been a Black skill, but the world around us demands we do this with more revolutionary intentions.

To avoid the pattern of simply reacting to the crises of our situation, we should engage in preemptive planning in order to move forward. Responses to our lack of health care, food, and housing are already happening in communities around the country. People are creating mutual aid groups, planting gardens, caring for one another, and sharing funds to support each other's needs. We can begin to organize these efforts to form an economy of interconnected communities and efforts to counteract the neglect and violence of the state. Though it is not particularly radical, crowdsourcing is another example of how people come together to survive. However, put into a different perspective, crowdfunding is a helpful way to help more people understand the importance of survival programs. Crowdfunding is often about us sustaining someone or something ourselves. Framed as a temporary measure until we've created something bigger and better, it can become a way to highlight an intentional community practice. This could potentially help people understand what the Panthers meant by "survival pending revolution." We can work together to meet each other's needs and accomplish more far-reaching goals in the same way to make social gains. We must see it as a transitional practice tied to a much larger transformative vision.

Abolition is part of that goal, but we must be wary and also specific about what we're abolishing and *why*. Not everyone who says they're an abolitionist even knows what the term means. Its increasing popularity risks stripping it of all meaning. If we allow it to become co-opted, it could easily become a reinvented version of reformism. According to Joy James, this narrowing of the meaning of abolition is "the logical conclusion of deradicalizing the prison struggle by severing it from a grassroots, working-class, Black base or people of color base that sought autonomy from the state."[26] The abolition that I am thinking of is that which seeks autonomy and ultimately the upending of the illegitimate state itself.

I first came across the term "abolition" in the writings of Angela Davis, who asked, in her work *Are Prisons Obsolete?*, whether prisons should be reformed or whether they should be abolished. She speaks to the risks, dangers, and advances of what's known as the prison industrial complex, the interlocked institutions responsible for the monumental growth of mass incarceration, the widespread confinement of people to benefit the corporations and state entities that create the unlivable conditions we endure every day. Davis writes: "Prison abolitionists are dismissed as utopians and idealists whose ideas are at best unrealistic and impracticable, and, at worst, mystifying and foolish. This is a measure of how difficult it is to envision a social order that does not rely on the threat of sequestering people in dreadful places designed to separate them from their communities and families. The prison is considered so 'natural' that it is extremely hard to imagine life without it."[27]

So, in addition to the challenge of abolitionism being stripped of

[26] Joy James, "The Architects of Abolitionism: George Jackson, Angela Davis, and the Deradicalization of Prison Struggles," talk given at Brown University, May 6, 2019, www.youtube.com/watch?v=z9rvRsWKDxo.

[27] Angela Davis, *Are Prisons Obsolete?* (New York: Seven Stories Press, 2003), 9.

meaning, there is the challenge of convincing people abolition is desirable in the first place. There can be no true push to abolish *anything* if we do not foreground the demand for autonomy in an anti-state abolition that draws from Black anarchisms. Amid our everyday struggle to live and get closer to a freedom we've never known, much of what we have known will have to be uprooted. The violence we've grown accustomed to, which many would rather accept than challenge, out of a fear of the unknown, can and must be obliterated. This is not an overnight process, but each and every night ahead of us is filled with the opportunity to act.

To understand clearly what are we abolishing and why, we must go deeper and confront concepts and behavior all too common among people in the midst of these struggles. The oppressive structures around us, like the police, the imperialist military, and the murderous courts, can be removed more expediently if we simultaneously address some of contradictions that plague us as we work for a better world. People have different visions of how to escape the disastrous violence of oppression, and some hope to buy their way out or return to pasts that may not be theirs to claim. If it's not the vote or reforming systemic problems that will aid us, some believe in reframing history in misleading ways. But in order to arrive at an effective revolutionary abolition capable of defeating oppressive authorities, we must delegitimize certain beliefs we hold within. These beliefs involve histories, mythologies, dogmas, and hierarchies that have nothing to contribute to our struggle.

CHAPTER TWO

ENDING ROYALTY, FAME, AND CELEBRITY

Do you know why people like me are shy about being capitalists?
Well, it's because we, for as long as we have known you, were
capital, like bales of cotton and sacks of sugar, and you were the
commanding, cruel capitalists, and the memory of this is so strong,
the experience so recent, that we can't quite bring ourselves to
embrace this idea that you think so much of. As for what we were
like before we met you, I no longer care. No periods of time over
which my ancestors held sway, no documentation of complex
civilisations, is any comfort to me. —Jamaica Kincaid

Part of struggling is learning, is studying. My own experiences
in the sixties led me to understand that it wasn't just enough to
ask for a piece of the pie. The whole liberation of oppressed
people in the United States had to do not with climbing up
some ladder to success, not for asking to be just like Rockefeller,
or just like Dupont, or just like Ford, because that would only
continue the oppression and exploitation of oppressed people
in the United States, and specifically African people
born and raised in the United States. —Assata Shakur

It's been clear for generations now that one of the central barriers to overcoming our oppressive conditions is the popular idea of success. The notion that if we work hard enough things will be fine clouds the reality: under capitalism, in order to be at the top, many others have to be on the bottom. How we define liberation and freedom matters, and the fact that many people have been deceived into thinking accumulating vast amounts of wealth or fame means being free is something we must combat. Royalty, fame, and celebrity to some degree dictate power in this society, but they are not liberation and can never bring freedom. Believing this myth feeds into a form of counterrevolution that the state uses to stabilize itself and keep people invested in its existence. If it's the state that we must unravel to achieve liberation, then we must take away the weapons it uses against us externally and internally. Deeper observation instructs us to not only think past these things in the present but also in our understanding of the past.

Since we live in a society in which virtually everything revolves around money, our relations to one another often mimic the exploitative logic that reigns over us. If you've ever been poor, been down bad, and been in the mud, perhaps it's made you so upset that you wish money didn't even exist. On the other hand, plenty of people believe that by achieving personal wealth they can trickle some of it down to others, "giving back to the community" and "raising people up." For them, philanthropic giving is the way for us to achieve some sort of freedom. They hope to become billionaires, oligarchs, and damn near royalty as a way out of the hell so many of us are trapped in. Of course, most of us will never achieve such wealth because it's already being hoarded by those who control it presently, the ruling class. The desire to be wealthy poses a barrier to collective liberation, allowing capitalistic relations to infect our movements. Even those who don't necessarily think money is the way out often place themselves in proximity to celebrities, wealth, and institutions that do. True liberation calls for the much-needed abolition of poverty *and* oppressive wealth, which requires an end to the compromising relationships our movements have with fortune.

For those of us whose ancestors were enslaved, there is a very troublesome aspect to all this. As people descended from those who were designated property, we are still treated with a disrespect that seems almost inescapable. Often, people long to recover their connection to the past, to know more about ancestry and the experiences of those who had virtually everything about their identity violently suppressed. This may lead some people to create their own polished versions of our history. Like the mainstream movement narratives that minimize Black radicalism in favor of reformism, some selective versions of Black history prioritize mythological tales of African royalty and African homogeneity. There is, I believe, a very close connection between this and positive attitudes toward individual accumulation of wealth.

For generations, Black America has heard a wide range of stories about how we ended up in the United States. Black movements like those led by the Nation of Islam have taken a religious approach to tackling our origins, while others have sought to uncover our supposedly universally aristocratic and royal genealogies. The narrative that we are all descended "from kings and queens" is disturbing. Emphasizing African royalty as something to take pride in reproduces the notion that wealth and power is what determines a person's value. Even if the kingdoms whose rulers we all supposedly descend from predate capitalism, they still contained relations in which hierarchy and domination gave people their value. It was putting a monetary value on people's heads that drove slavers to put people into chains in the first place. Feeding into this sort of irrationality will not free us of them.

At various times, we've seen the odd embrace of Egypt as a main source of our Black origins and the great neglect of the actual places where our ancestors primarily come from. West-Central Africa, Senegambia, and other important locations that the Atlantic slave trade prioritized are regularly ignored by those who choose to embrace fictional origins. Our lives are not fairy tales. The fact that we've been inundated with media that glorify the supposed magic of royalty may be partially to blame, but dealing with such mystification requires us to travel across time, place, and status to see ourselves more clearly in the present.

Undoubtedly, one reason people want to believe we're all descended from royalty is due to an aversive reaction to oppression and subjugation. Our inability to acquire full citizenship has helped mischaracterize Black people as a people without culture or origins. Despite the monumental achievements of enslaved Africans to not only survive the Middle Passage but also innovate, invent, and establish themselves in an unfamiliar land, there are efforts to define Black people through the priorities of capitalism. Attempts to feel better about ourselves shouldn't rely on narratives that side with oppression and dominance. We don't need to portray ourselves or our lineage in relation to royalty to show we're worthy of respect. We already are, as people, deserving of dignity, without laying claim to some hierarchical position within a nation, kingdom, or tribe. The desire to depict Black people as estimable through wealth and nobility in response to racism is self-defeating.

Reliance on stratification and terror, on ranking human beings, fed into the slave trade that in turn became an engine of capitalism. We need to collectively interrogate our own origins in these violent circumstances. There certainly *are* some Black people in the United States who can legitimately claim some sort of royal heritage, but that's an unreliable foundation for resistance in the present. Even if there were those who fought the transatlantic slave trade while defending kingdoms and dynasties on the African continent, structures they were defending aren't necessarily ours to claim now. We should be able to appreciate the complexity of why some people rebelled in favor of those structures, while being critical and true to our politics, which might not agree with such things today. Black populations throughout the Americas are made up of people descended from those who could have *already* been servants, prisoners, and slaves in the lands they were taken from, before arrival. Imagine if their versions of citizenship or belonging were already compromised. Many of us could be descended from someone who was subjugated in their homeland before being forced to come here to face a new form of subjugation, only for us to pretend they were of some royal bloodline to serve our own fairy tale.

"I laugh at my former childish fantasies," writes the great poet Aimé Césaire:

> No, we've never been Amazons of the king of Dahomey, nor princes of Ghana with eight hundred camels, nor wise men in Timbuktu under Askia the Great, nor the architects of Djenné, nor Madhis, nor warriors. We don't feel under our armpit the itch of those who in the old days carried a lance. And since I have sworn to leave nothing out of our history (I who love nothing better than a sheep grazing his own afternoon shadow), I may as well confess that we were at all times pretty mediocre dishwashers, shoeblacks without ambition, at best conscientious sorcerers.[1]

[1] Aimé Césaire, *Notebook of a Return to the Native Land* (Middletown, CT: Wesleyan University Press, 2001), 27.

This shouldn't be taken as an insult. What *is* disrespectful, though, is assigning all our ancestors a royal status, thereby erasing many lived realities in order to make ourselves feel better at their expense. In any case, Black Americans must confront the truths about who we actually are *now* rather than fabricating counterproductive tales about who we were *then*. The weight of the oppression we endure today will not be lifted by reaffirming the same falsehoods—about success, about what constitutes power, about raising ourselves above others—that have forged the steel of cages we have yet to break free from.

What if our ancestors hated the very sorts of people some work to try to turn them into? What if we're descended from people we wouldn't necessarily be proud of, people who did horrible things? There is no single, uniform rendering of the ancestors. Any attempt to create one is misleading, if not an outright fabrication. Hortense Spillers made a stunning point about this in Arthur Jafa's film, *Dreams Are Colder than Death*:

> What I say is that this oedipal crisis gets buried in Middle Passage. And that going back to confront the fathers who put us in the trade would be to confront an original sin, the relationship to the past, to the fathers, to the ancestors. "Some of you helped to put me here." How do we solve that, or how are we going to talk about it? The problem is intramural, rather than cross-racial. Fundamentally an intramural problem between generations of Africans. And . . . the slave trade gets in there,

turns the picture around, and somehow we've got to find our way back to this original dilemma, what we think of as a crime. And not a lot of people want to talk about it. The slave trade required European and African operatives, and you're never going to tell me a different thing.[2]

The evils of slavery can be addressed without assigning grandiose characteristics to our ancestry. We don't have to pretend that a horrific situation wasn't complicated. It absolutely was. There was collaboration between Africans and Europeans to enslave rivals, enemies, and prisoners. That's a known fact, but my interest here is analyzing how intentional mis-remembering can affect the present. Overlooking the dangerousness of the modes of domination that collaborated with the slave trade is risky. This narrative that we are royalty fallen from grace may actually help maintain certain forms of oppression. It's a form of thinking that does nothing to threaten the capitalistic terror of the state. The idea that someone's worth is dependent on status or class or hierarchy needs to be done away with completely, not restored to a past form. The legacy of this sort of rationale and how it manifests today endangers us by affirming the false reasoning of an egregious empire. There is also a deeper, more insidious racial logic involved that we can see all around us now.

Wanting to know where we come from feeds into the burgeoning genealogy industry. Popular "ancestry services" capitalize on Black

[2] *Dreams Are Colder than Death*, directed by Arthur Jafa (Los Angeles: TNEG, 2014).

A performer at a slave rebellion reenactment stops to rest

people and a sense of loss around the ruptures caused by enslavement. Dorothy Roberts has written at length about how this big business reinforces mythology about race and biology: "Telling customers that they are a composite of several broad anthropological groupings reinforces three central myths about race: that there are pure races, that each race contains people who are fundamentally the same and fundamentally different from people in other races, and that races can be biologically demarcated. The concept of dividing a person's genotype into racial components assumes that each component is racially pure. We can only imagine someone to be a quarter European if we have a concept of someone who is 100 percent European."[3]

Roberts goes on to mention the research of Alondra Nelson, a sociologist who writes in detail about this. Nelson has addressed Black people's "affiliative self-fashioning" and "genealogical aspirations." In the article "Bio Science: Genetic Genealogy Testing and the Pursuit of African Ancestry," she writes, "Testing promises to reveal elusive knowledge, yet the particular longings that root-seekers of African descent seem to feel when they resort to it are shaped by distinct histories of slavery and the continuing realities of racial oppression. Root-seekers' sense of autonomy and empowerment may come at the cost of acquiescence to a classificatory logic of hu-

[3] Dorothy E. Roberts, *Fatal Invention: How Science, Politics, and Big Business Re-create Race in the Twenty-First Century* (New York: New Press, 2012), 228.

man types that compounds, rather than challenges, social inequality. The affiliative self-fashioning described here is then a limited type of agency, unfolding from within less mutable social structures."[4] In a *New York Times* op-ed, she is even more definitive:

> The truth is that sets of DNA markers cannot tell us who we really are because genetic data is technical and identity is social. The science in question is a form of chromosome mapping similar to that used in the billion-dollar genetic ancestry testing industry in the United States. That testing draws on incomplete data about human genetic diversity. . . . When we're faced with difficult issues about the past that bear on the present, it is tempting to take these tests as proof of identity. But these genetic tests cannot confirm social dynamics. Identity is socially, politically and legally determined, even if shaped by genetics. Yet, genetic ancestry testing does not offer insights about these dynamics. So, we can't look to DNA to settle debates about identity.[5]

[4] Alondra Nelson, "Bio Science: Genetic Genealogy Testing and the Pursuit of African Ancestry," *Social Studies of Science* 38, no. 5 (2008): 776.

[5] Alondra Nelson, "Elizabeth Warren and the Folly of Genetic Ancestry Tests," *New York Times*, October 17, 2018. Nelson was responding to claims from Senator Elizabeth Warren that her DNA was analyzed, proving she has Native American ancestry. Nelson points out that Indigenous communities have refused to take part in genetic data-gathering efforts done at the behest of researchers and commercial entities. They did this to resist reducing Native culture, identity, and history to a matter of genetics, when it is something instead recognized through sovereign tribal authority.

These points may be lost on those who want to escape into an identity they feel affirms something deep within them. Nelson concludes, "This is also worrisome because the social life of DNA, the ability of DNA to be used in ways other than its original intent, is moving into the criminal justice system and elsewhere, as the recent uses of the family history website GEDmatch and other genealogical databases show. We should resist the pressure to publicly disclose our personal genetic information."[6]

The desire to know more about our origins runs the risk of compromising our relationship to historical fact, reaffirms white supremacist and capitalist rationales, and threatens our privacy, all to gather dubious information. Here, Frantz Fanon comes to mind: "In no way should I dedicate myself to the revival of an unjustly unrecognized Negro civilization. I will not make myself the man of any past. I do not want to exalt the past at the expense of my present and of my future."[7] Who we are shouldn't be a difficult question with such a rich heritage visible all around us. The anarchistic aspects of so many Black experiences are something we can come to embrace, something that can fill voids rather than create them. Though we have been wronged and are still being harmed, being Black is not an injury or an insult. While confirming things about

[6] Ibid.

[7] Frantz Fanon, *Black Skin, White Masks* (London: Pluto Press, 2008), 176.

our pasts could be satisfying, it's not guaranteed to heal what has been broken. Chasing royal associations and today's desire to be a "king" or a "queen" has direct ties to the misery that capitalism inflicts on our day-to-day lives.

The ruling class is treated like kings and queens, and among them are the celebrity elite that get worshipped by adoring fans playing the role of loyal subjects. Whether playful or not, there are serious consequences of such devotion. We've seen the influence of fame used to endorse terrible people and terrible causes, especially in the realm of electoral politics, where celebrities' fame is used to bolster one ruling-class party or another. Repetitive, failed reform efforts and voting drives have consistently used popularity and fame to funnel people back into the ineffective, temporary, and symbolic methods we have been indoctrinated into thinking are the only ways to transform our lives for the better. Politicians and administrators of the state are shielded by the endorsements of celebrities and even highly visible activists who legitimize them. The manipulation of desire and the public adoration of celebrity always involves fanciful dreams of domination and control. This emotional turmoil ultimately helps justify the existence of a ruling class and the state.

There will always be those who long to be one of the rich and famous instead of struggling to abolish conditions that create haves and have nots. But fantasies like this forget or repress the obvious truth that wealth cannot exist without poverty. The project of accumulating wealth is called exploitation, making more from some-one's labor than you pay them in wages. It is the result of workers being used and overworked. Of course, under capitalism, every commodity is born of exploitation that the ruling class tries to make increasingly acceptable to consumers. In our technology filled with conflict minerals, our food grown by abused farmworkers, and most other items around us, there is someone's suffering.

The wealthy flaunt what they amass so that we're reminded of what we don't have and what we need to supposedly work hard to get—as if most of us aren't already working incredibly hard. But this idea that everyone who's wealthy labored to become so is absurd and easily disproved. Wealth is regularly inherited and passed down, just as in the feudal regimes that are supposed to be a thing of the past. Their money increases by percentage points without them working to make it happen. Yet we are somehow expected to believe that these people deserve to live longer, better, happier lives. What of the countless teachers, construction workers, miners, drivers, servers, maids, janitors, sex workers, cooks, electricians, plumbers, mothers, and other workers who tirelessly keep this society going every single day for meager earnings (if they receive any earnings at all)? Don't they work hard? Let the people who collect the garbage of a wasteful society stop for a week, and watch the world begin to slowly fall apart.

What convinces people to accept these class divisions? One obvious cause is the endless stream of media glorifying money and endless riches, while insulting the poor. The desire to become part of the ruling and/or celebrity class infects even the most oppressed people.

The same ideology is pushed by Black capitalists, who take advantage of this mentality to chastise Black people who don't have as much as them and who must therefore be lazy or undisciplined. Anti-Black racism, even when parroted by Black people, designates those suffering from poverty as incapable and unequipped, while ignoring the systemic violence of white supremacy. These ideas have a long history, going back past President Ronald Reagan's myth of the "welfare queen," past the 1965 Moynihan report on Black poverty, all the way to slavery. They rely on the assumption that we are incapable because we were meant to be in bondage as subjects, not free people with any true agency. Supposedly, when we're not in bondage we don't know what to do with ourselves.

Every Black person in the United States is told these mistruths—to the point that some of us tell them ourselves. Some try to escape by making themselves into royalty through capital, so they can victim-blame like any other capitalist. Wealthy Black people, elite celebrities, businesspeople, politicians, clergy, and others recycle narratives that perpetuate white supremacist myths that we need management. They use their established positions to reduce Black people to a lost herd requiring a shepherd. In fact, their positions of relative power and wealth are aided by any of us who would believe in and affirm the rigid hierarchies they represent. The white ruling class, of course, does what's needed to support this arrangement, situating these manifestations of a Black bourgeoisie as de facto "community leaders."

The Black elite are good at making people believe in them, and they have the capital to help. The more fame or money you have, the more you're a supposed expert on all things Black. It's been happening long enough to have been addressed and called out many times in our history. In a 1963 interview at the University of California, Malcolm X (el-Hajj Malik el-Shabazz) once said: "Comedians, comics, trumpet players, baseball players. Show me in the white community where a comedian is a white leader. Show me in the white community where a singer is a white leader or a dancer or a trumpet player is a white leader. These aren't leaders. These are puppets and clowns that have been set up over the Black community by the white community and have been made celebrities and usually they say exactly what they know the white man wants to hear."[8]

Malcolm's rebuttal of a *Newsweek* poll in this case highlights an important point. The entire notion of the necessity of "leadership"

[8] Malcolm X, "Interview at University of California, Berkeley, October 11, 1963," video, archive.org/details/CSPAN3_20150301_161000_1963_Interview_With_Malcolm_X.

in charismatic and messianic forms is absurd.[9] Why do we never refer to "white leaders?" The very question would seem perplexing to most people. Yet Black people are no more inherently infantile or in need of guidance by so-called Black leaders. Those leaders do, however, serve a purpose in maintaining the very power structures we should hope to abolish in liberatory efforts. In reality, our lives require inventing and mastering modes of survival that may not be required of others, and we do so without being led. The fact that we can be targeted by the state at *any* moment tasks Black people with becoming adept at avoiding brutality every single day. However, it's in the best interest of the ruling class to keep Black people from realizing that we don't need divine deliverance, royalty, or leaders.

Over a decade after Malcolm X criticized Black celebrities as puppets, artist and cultural activist Camille Yarbrough released an album titled *The Iron Pot Cooker*.[10] This debut was based on

[9] See Cedric Robinson, "Malcolm Little as a Charismatic Leader," in *On Racial Capitalism, Black Internationalism, and Cultures of Resistance*, edited by H. L. T. Quan (London: Pluto Press, 2019). Robinson analyzes Malcolm X's charismatic leadership through a psychohistorical approach. He highlights that, although Malcolm was certainly right in pointing out who was not a leader, he himself engaged at times in methods that I hope to trouble in this book.

[10] Camille Yarbrough, *The Iron Pot Cooker* (Vanguard, 1975), rereleased on CD in 1999.

Point Comfort at Fort Monroe in Hampton,
Virginia. The site of the 1619 landing

Yarbrough's one-woman spoken-word show, now put to music, and it includes themes relating to race, class, and gender. Two tracks in particular have helped me think through the question of Black leadership.

The first is a medley titled "Dream / Panic / Sonny Boy the Rip-Off Man / Little Sally the Super Sex Star (Taking Care of Business)." A slow-moving introduction describing the Black experience in the United States shifts into the hectic second section, "Panic." Here Yarbrough dashes over a pulsing melody with a laundry list of troubles ("our panic"), like houselessness, domestic violence, unemployment, and incarceration. As she begins the transition into the third part, she calls "Look out for number one panic!" and repeats "Get them before they get me." The music becomes circus-like, and she emulates a ringmaster, shouting "Ladies and gentlemen and children of all ages, hurry, hurry, hurry! Come see the freaks in their ghetto colony cages!"

The main event of the freak show, and the center of the song's third section, is Sonny Boy the Rip-Off Man. "Just wave a dollar in front of his face," Yarbrough says, before outlining the tragedy of this character. He is someone who will seemingly do anything to get money and celebrity. "He'll push, he'll pimp, he'll run a game, make a name, get that glory, get that fame," she says; "he's trying to find some way in the plan, some way already decided not by him, but for him." Sonny Boy, whom she describes as a "programmed, computerized, colonized, dehumanized, guaranteed-to-self-destruct, rip-off man," is a spectacle, desperately chasing fame and capital at any cost. He is "programmed to think that, if he wants to win, he has to rip off your mother, your father, your sister, your brother." The lives of other Black people are "the price that he pays for his custom-made cars, for his programmed ego trip." While Yarbrough's character is clearly a manifestation of common hustlers and scammers, he is also an indictment of Black capitalism. He represents what has long been labeled and derided as a "poverty pimp," one of the grifting preachers, shady activists, and would-be leaders who exploit serious issues for their own personal benefit and brand building. This passionate song is a denunciation of the desire to put accumulation before the lives of our fellow Black people in an obsessive drive to escape individual oppression through exploitative wealth. The last part of the song includes the chorus, "That's what we call takin' care of business / That's what we call doin' our thing / Trying to get away from being hungry / Trying to enjoy what money can bring."

The final track on *The Iron Pot Cooker* is the stunning "All Hid." The song's urgency is etched in sharp lyrics and brilliant production. Yarbrough again takes several shots at Black capitalism in the face of widespread poverty: "One, two, three, four / People get tired of being poor / Five, ten, fifteen, twenty / Why you so mad when you got plenty?" That the song's title refers to the mystification of class relations in the Black community becomes clear when Yarbrough smacks her lips and repeats "all hid" several times before confronting the wealthy Black elite: "Now sellin' their souls across the nation / Living in high-rise isolation / Making obsolete two-cent deals / Being lubricating grease for the system's wheels." The music gradually increases in tempo, and Yarbrough painstakingly reminds us that the problem of the Black elite isn't new: "In the name of class, they sell their race and cut off their nose to spite their face / In their high-heeled shoes, they're claiming class, while damning the folks still in the grass." All of this, including how blame is placed, as she says, on the "lazy welfare bums," is disturbingly prescient, even if more people seem to have bought into the deception.

An artistic testimony created in the shadow of the Nixon presidency, *The Iron Pot Cooker* is more than a classic album. Its relevance here underscores a time period leading up to when Lorenzo Kom'boa Ervin would write *Anarchism and the Black Revolution* while imprisoned in 1979. Ervin's intervention indicated disillusionment with the failures of Black leadership during this period. Black movements were vulnerable to a wide array of attacks from the highest offices in the country, including attempts that would exploit Black leadership, capital, and celebrity. President Nixon championed Black capitalism as a means for Black people's self-sufficiency. Today the Black elite, their followers, and others who may not realize it parrot Nixonian talking points when they proclaim the gospel of Black capitalism. From James Brown to Jay-Z, there is a legacy of Black celebrities profiting off pro-Black messages while being conservative and business-minded in the most self-serving of ways. They endorse the thinking that reduces many Black people to ignorant underachievers seeking handouts. Robert L. Allen, referring to his book *Black Awakening in Capitalist America*, summarizes his appraisal of this dynamic: "I argued that the rhetoric of black capitalism was politically motivated as a way of steering the black power movement in a capitalist direction and undermining the influence of black radicals. I argued that black capitalism was largely an illusion, that small black businesses could not compete with enormous white corporations economically. I argued that black capitalism was insubstantial, and not likely to survive the harsh wind of recession."[11]

Black capitalism, and the celebrity and fame that feed into it, are dangerous infiltrators of our movements. For decades, we have battled internally with these issues, watching as activists become celebrities in their own right. They rise up to become very visible, unelected spokespeople and pundits. Leaders become famous, and the famous become leaders, and all of them cozy up to the establishment. Much like people who enter positions of relative power as the result of diversity initiatives within the institutions that do us harm, these leader-celebrities (or celebrity-leaders) become representa-

[11] Robert L. Allen, "Reassessing the Internal (Neo) Colonialism Theory," *Black Scholar* 35, no. 1 (2005): 5.

tives of *all* Black people. When something terrible happens, they are brought out to comment, provide insight, and speak for everyone by drawing from their bottomless wells of expertise. They're directly related to the disingenuous nonprofits and foundations with missions to tackle problems they have no interest in actually solving because their living depends on the problem continuing. Their seat at the table allows them to make, or at least influence, decisions on behalf of Black America. That seat and that table must be smashed, and the house they are in must be demolished.

It is sad to see how charismatic and famous activists—leftist, liberal, and otherwise—have positioned themselves as a sort of vanguard whose celebrity is supposed to be a win for us all. Their awards, notoriety, profiles, and proximity to power, not to mention their wealth, are supposed to be a victory for the movement. In reality, they organize nothing and therefore can win nothing. They must invent victories, and we are supposed to take pride in symbolic wins. The people occupying these high positions in white supremacist society are safety valves to quell Black uprising and complaints. We are all supposed to be happy because "one of us" made it. However, what does any of this matter if *where* they're making it is a place that needs to be completely torn down? Abolition demands that we not sit by hoping for a chosen few to make it inside any institution that will ultimately change them and not be fundamentally changed by them, as history has shown us countless times before.

Celebrity, like royalty or any feudal rank, doesn't make anyone

essentially more special or deserving. Divorced from the daily struggles of Black people and positioned in proximity to the white power
structure, their opinions should be judged according to their sincer-
ity and relevance, not their visibility. Certainly, there are entertainers and artists who worked very hard to become known for their
craft. There are also many activists who accomplished important
things before they gained notoriety. That's not to say we shouldn't
be fans of entertainers, athletes, or performers. Our favorite movies,
shows, or pieces of art are not suddenly invalidated by the fame of
their creators. The issue is that notoriety, fame, and capital can
share a common thread of exclusion. They regularly center the individual instead of the collective, and true liberation is a collective
matter. Some people will always have extraordinary talents or gifts
that others don't, but that doesn't mean that they deserve mansions
while others, not far away, are unhoused and vulnerable. Those
mansions and the lifestyles they shelter come at the expense of others. The argument that the rich and famous provide goals for Black
people to aspire to, like the anyone-can-be-president mythology of
the two-party system, relies on a very narrow and individualized
idea of freedom. Joining the ranks of one's oppressors is not freedom.
And, for the rest of us, oppression at the hands of someone who
looks like us is no more acceptable.

People can be famous and attempt to leverage that fame for good.
A notable example of a celebrity who worked to use visibility to

fight for Black people to such an extent that it put his own life in jeopardy is Paul Robeson. He was an iconic athlete, actor, singer, scholar, lawyer, and world-famous activist who fought tirelessly for the rights of many internationally. His wide range of abilities offered him fame in several arenas, especially for a Black man of his time (he was born in 1898). Robeson spoke out against fascism during the Spanish Civil War stating, "The artist must take sides. He must elect to fight for freedom or for slavery. I have made my choice. I had no alternative. The history of this era is characterized by the degradation of my people."[12] His work even took him to the United Nations, where he aided the delivery of the petition titled "We Charge Genocide: The Crime of Government Against the Negro People," detailing the wide variety of ways that state violence worked through lynching, brutality, and abandonment to destroy Black America. Robeson once said, "I am a Negro with every drop of my blood and with every stir of my soul.... In my Negro heart lies buried the memories of centuries of oppression."[13] Robeson was an advocate for workers and the causes of oppressed people worldwide, and he was targeted by anticommunists for his associations with the Soviet Union. Shana L. Redmond has described a crucial

[12] Phillip Foner, ed., *Paul Robeson Speaks* (New York: Citadel Press, 1978), 119.

[13] Harold D. Weaver, "Paul Robeson and The Pan-African World," *Présence Africaine* 107 (1978): 217.

observation of Robeson's "forced assimilation" that should not be neglected: "The wide sociopolitical cleavage between his political virtues and those of the nation are made seamless . . . in an effort to so intimately tie them together that one might lose sight of the fact that . . . as much as he loved any number of imagined communities of which he'd become a fixture, Paul was a steward of no nation. He dreamed of 'autonomy rather than nationhood' and forged his allegiance in struggle with people and ideas, not states."[14]

Robeson presents an understanding that is not just important for celebrities but also for all of us striving for more. His clarity around the broken promises of citizenship as a Black person from the United States informed a worldview that disregarded borders and the bro-

---

[14] Shana L. Redmond, *Everything Man: The Form and Function of Paul Robeson* (Durham, NC: Duke University Press, 2020), 87. Redmond was referring to how Robeson essentially became a "noncitizen ambassador" in national service to Wales. She points out how his historical legacy and association with Wales are used "from beyond the grave." Her point applies widely to how celebrities, leaders, and others like him are attached to national causes and objectified by state projects. Still, Robeson did not completely escape criticisms of celebrity and charismatic leadership. It can be argued that he put himself in a position for this to happen through the romanticization of state projects like the Soviet Union. For a more critical portrait of Robeson and other celebrities I've referenced like Lorraine Hansberry, see Harold Cruse's *The Crisis of the Negro Intellectual* (New York: Morrow, 1967). Cruse challenges the class background, motivations, and leftwing dogma of Black celebrities who are now highly (and often uncritically) regarded in Black history.

ken promises of the United States itself. His international work highlights the global nature of an ongoing fight against colonialism and imperialism. This is important because in the details of these understandings is the truth that, just as we shouldn't seek celebrity or charismatic and messianic forms of leadership, we shouldn't idealize other nations using these same justifications. Robeson himself can be and is intentionally misremembered in service to national causes that may not completely capture his complexity.

Fred Hampton, deputy chairman of the Black Panthers, once said, "We don't hate the white people; we hate the oppressor, whether he be white, black, brown, or yellow."[15] He was talking about the need to counter the idea that just because someone is Black they are loyal to the cause of Black liberation. He explicitly told us that we would not fight capitalism with "Black capitalism" and identified the threat the latter posed to Black people. Hampton condemned the fallacy of attempting to reinvent ourselves by trying to gain access to this violent domination.

The time we spend dreaming about fame, celebrity, and royalty is a reflection of our own class politics. Ultimately, only collective strength will help build new and effective movements. As Ella Baker once said, "strong people don't need strong leaders." Hierarchical

[15] *The Murder of Fred Hampton*, directed by Howard Alk (Chicago: Facets Multimedia, 1971).

domination can always get in the way. The revolutionary movement to abolish empire should be rooted in education and truth, not personalities. That's how we will trouble the institutions of normalcy and make oppression unacceptable.

In order to strengthen movements, there must also be a radical honesty about the moments that came before us. We can't learn from failures unless they are recognized as failures in the first place. In the next chapter, I will look at what I see as the religiosity of what gets called the "left," something I think has long been a burdensome, counterproductive problem. We have many of the most crucial insights needed for revolutionary abolitionist struggle, but we are often stuck in the battles and personalities of the past. In many ways this involves the sort of fantasies, fetishization, and celebrity worship that I've described in this chapter. In order to see clearly, we must be willing to do the work of internal critique and surpass the shortcomings of the past instead of mimicking or worshiping them.

CHAPTER THREE

THE SANCTIMONIOUS LEFT

*What name do you give to the nature of the Universe? There are
some realms in which names, nomination, is premature. My only
loyalties are to the morally just world; and my happiest and
most stunning opportunity for raising hell with corruption and
deceit are with other Black people. I suppose that makes me a
part, an expression, of Black Radicalism.* —Cedric Robinson

What good is idealizing a revolutionary or radical past if it doesn't
direct you to action in the present? How we relate to history may
dictate our contemporary efforts to advance a liberatory movement.
People and projects can become so wrapped up in the story of their
past that they cannot see how it has become a hindrance to securing
a better future. In the previous two chapters, I've tried to make this
point as it relates to the idea of Black citizenship in the United
States as well as to the fantastical narratives we tell ourselves in response to our compromised position. Now I want to look at another
area where fictions and distortions regularly prevent us from imag-
ining real liberation because they confine us with a particular image

of themselves. This has been the plight of "the left" for quite some time.

In the United States there often seems to be a lot of confusion around who is and who isn't on the left. The label of "leftist" is applied and misapplied regularly. This is done out of ignorance much of the time, but it's also a symptom of the lack of an actual left to identify. In a country that's overwhelmingly right-wing, this is unsurprising. The lack of an *actual* leftist political opposition— by which I mean one that is a proactively organized, revolutionary threat—plagues us. One of the two reigning political parties entertains members masquerading as a "left" opposition, when the party itself is only a different tool of state oppression. What we need is a strong internal analysis and critique of who we are, who we struggle alongside, and whose interests contradict our goals. When we look closely, we will find that even the left is distorted by cultism, patriotism, and the sort of fetishistic fandom I described in chapter 2.

Mythology can have its uses in bringing people together around common causes. As I've mentioned, it can be a response to oppression that's used to motivate people. It's not inherently negative, but much of the mythology and doctored narratives I want to point out here certainly are. Important questions raised by Cedric Robinson can help us interrogate several aspects of what we may encounter confronting the past and our perception of it:

Is it coincidence that what we now instruct ourselves to know about human society, in particular its structures (its political systems, its orderings) and its vital systemic principle (its *sine qua non*, political authority), is very much like what we have been told to know through the archaicisms of cosmogonic myths, theogonic fables, folk-stories, oral and literary traditions? I think not. Is it that regardless of the changing natures of heroes or principal actors, we have compulsively come to associate them with authorships? That is, whether these figures are in nature divine, mortal, or something in between, that when we think about them, ritually or reasonably, in myth or in analysis, we are celebrating them—celebrating their authority over life and death.[1]

In a country where taking basic steps to improve social welfare and provide for people in need is seen as "radical," the left has been pummeled by the state. Its history is filled with assassination, coups, raids, imprisonment, and executions. The relentless U.S. government has taken countless opportunities to destroy leftist movements and kill the people associated with them, within its borders and abroad. As a response, leftists have worked hard to disprove and overcome the lies of state propaganda and oppressive retellings of historical events. We know that, as C. L. R. James told us, "The

[1] Cedric Robinson, *The Terms of Order: Political Science and the Myth of Leadership*, new ed. (Chapel Hill: University of North Carolina Press, 2016), 124.

only place where Negroes did not revolt is in the pages of capitalist historians."[2] And it's knowing this that leads us to resist efforts to downplay and erase the glorious rebellions and revolutions of our past. However, when resisting ruling-class narratives edges over into hagiography and zealotry, as it often does, we must stop and reassess.

It is always good to remember and reflect on past movements, but they don't necessarily always lead to the new political formations we need today. Believing that we can transpose the actions of our predecessors into the present is a problem not limited to any one segment of the left, but how and why different camps engage in it is something we have to examine. One of the easiest identifiable iterations comes from those who are popularly denounced by anarchists, the authoritarian leftists. Founding Black anarchists and other Black leftists who defined various autonomous politics have long-standing issues with this segment of the left. Black anarchism itself represents divergence, evolution, and political movement away from it. Black anarchism is born out of a critique of Marxist-Leninists, Stalinists, and Maoists for the social relations that its originators formerly embraced under these terms. The problems of cultism, dogma, and dictatorial leadership are not new to the left.

[2] C. L. R. James (writing as J. R. Johnson), "The Revolution and the Negro," *New International* 5 (December 1939): 339.

Leftists become segmented into stagnant denominations incapable of effectively engaging and organizing among masses of different people, while glorifying and sanctifying historical figures who actually did.

Karl Marx understood that the struggle against religion is much deeper than simply opposing religious institutions. It is also "indirectly the struggle against that world whose spiritual aroma is religion."[3] What he saw as "the opium of the people" has an equally intoxicating effect on political organizations that situate themselves just as rigidly as conservative religious sects. For Marx, the comfort religion provides is based on people's understanding of the oppressive social and economic conditions they face. "To call them to give up their illusions about their conditions is to *call on them to give up a condition that requires illusions*."[4] Religion, or religiosity, isn't the

---

[3] Karl Marx, *Critique of Hegel's Philosophy of Right* (1844), excerpted in *Marx on Religion*, edited by John Raines (Philadelphia: Temple University Press, 2002), 171.

[4] Ibid. Although Marx was outspoken about religion and dogma at different times, he asserted his own work in a theological way. Many of Marx's most valuable insights and contributions are interrupted by this. His secular politics became doctrine through a self-selected "scientific" designation. This led to his most fervent followers treating his work as timelessly infallible. This way Marx's socialism becomes the *only* form of socialism, which has never been the case. As Cedric Robinson notes, "Marxism crafted a historical pedestal for itself by transmuting all previous and alternative socialisms into poorly detailed blueprints or dead-end

whole of the problem, but it does indicate and point us in the direction of necessary internal and external confrontations. The parts of the left that wallow in their own sectarian fervor are a glaring example of a lack of critical introspection.

Consciously or not, the leftist who works to obsessively trace and cement a revolutionary theogony relies on a bygone past to distract from present failures. Among authoritarian leftists especially, this transforms politics into secular religions. Further, any critique is seen as a form of religious persecution that "proves" one's critics are siding with the enemy—in this case, the police or government. Even internal criticism is smothered in favor of silent acceptance of dogma. However antireligious they imagine themselves, they treat their own political positions with the same unbending, uncompromising dedication that zealots bring to their faith. Sectarian infighting among leftists, authoritarian and otherwise, resembles faiths fighting in the name of their icons.

For newcomers to social and political movements, this can all be very intimidating. Unwittingly, passionate people become absorbed into stale sectarian conflicts, and, all the while, the state apparatus targets and crushes us. It undermines our struggles and makes us

---

protoforms of itself." Robinson explains traces of the gospel in Marxism as well as its own religiousness in lengthy detail in *An Anthropology of Marxism* (Chapel Hill: University of North Carolina Press, 2019).

susceptible to attacks by the right-wing forces. It also shrinks what could be a larger oppositional force to fight against white supremacy, the state, and fascism. While authoritarian leftists like this embody many of the worst aspects of the church, they do so without achieving nearly as much. Like churches that compete to grow their tithe-paying memberships, leftist organizations vie with one another for the minds and dues of devoted adherents. They fight for leadership over movements that they often did not spark and prematurely for political control of the postrevolutionary society they envision but consistently fail to materialize. However, their incessant bickering weakens movements to the point that *no one* can gain enough ground to topple the oppressive forces we're up against.

Also like many religious organizations, the authoritarian left often works under the influence of messianic modes of leadership. Its doctrine and beliefs work in favor of the notion that leadership shouldn't be challenged. Revolutionary heroes and leaders of the past are revered like gods, no matter their failures, shortcomings, or abuses of power. However much they condemned religion, dead and martyred revolutionaries become holy icons with followers who take on the names of the dead they venerate. Just as followers of Christ can label themselves Christians, the authoritarian leftist followers of diverging sects like those of Stalin and Trotsky become Stalinists and Trotskyists. These followers proselytize oppressed people, offering salvation, deliverance, and liberation, if only those they see as in need of their politics will fall into faithful practice. Challenging this sort of orthodoxy is one of the most important tasks we face.

"The tradition of all dead generations weighs like a nightmare on the brains of the living," writes Marx. "And just as they seem to be occupied with revolutionizing themselves and things, creating something that did not exist before, precisely in such epochs of revolutionary crisis they anxiously conjure up the spirits of the past to their service, borrowing from them names, battle slogans, and costumes in order to present this new scene in world history in time-honored disguise and borrowed language."[5] The anxiety that leftists feel as they face the task of creating something new leads them to reflexively embrace old and decaying political forms. Our response to this cannot involve more of the same. As Marx wrote to Arnold Ruge: "Our motto must therefore be: reform of consciousness not through dogmas, but by analyzing the mystical consciousness that is unintelligible to itself, whether it manifests itself in a religious or a political form."[6]

Authoritarian leftist hagiography is even more problematic and

[5] Karl Marx, *The Eighteenth Brumaire of Louis Bonaparte* (New York: International Publishers, 1963), 15.

[6] Karl Marx, "For a Ruthless Criticism of Everything Existing," letter to Arnold Ruge in the *Deutsch-Französosische Jahrbücher* in 1844, in *The Marx-Engels Reader*, edited by Robert Tucker (New York: W. W. Norton, 1978), 15.

dangerous when it becomes part of the nation-building process. The untouchable revolutionary heroes' ghosts are absorbed by states outside of the United States and are revered the way the "Founding Fathers" are revered within the U.S. borders. Certainly, the violence of the imperialist U.S. empire is in a category of its own, but a comparison between it and allegedly leftist governments is made necessary by the similar logics behind both and the danger of where this sort of thinking leads.

Revolutionary and nominally anti-imperialist leftist icons are conflated with the states they helped found, ruled over, or lived in. Their legacies are used to anthropomorphize structures that are state mechanisms and conflate governance with the dream of an accomplished revolution. Their actions become one with those states, granting governments a shared cloak of veneration as well as a humanity they rarely deserve. This shifting of allegiance from idolized individuals to the states that claim their legacy means defending the indefensible: state violence. Sectarianism levels up to international relations, clouding the judgment of leftists who bicker among themselves like sports fans whose teams are constantly losing. Political debates become justifications for other state atrocities, as we lose sight of our own struggles.

W. E. B. Du Bois discusses how ignoring history for the sake of glorifying the state plays out similarly in the United States in "The Propaganda of History," a chapter in *Black Reconstruction*:

If history is going to be scientific, if the record of human action is going to be set down with the accuracy and faithfulness of detail which will allow its use as a measuring rod and guidepost for the future of nations, there must be set some standards of ethics in research and interpretation.

If, on the other hand, we are going to use history for our pleasure and amusement, for inflating our national ego, and giving us a false but pleasurable sense of accomplishment, then we must give up the idea of history as a science or as an art using the results of science, and admit frankly that we are using a version of historic fact in order to influence and educate the new generation along the way we wish.

It is propaganda like this that has led men in the past to insist that history is "lies agreed upon"; and to point out the danger in such misinformation. It is indeed extremely doubtful if any permanent benefit comes to the world through such action. Nations reel and stagger on their way; they make hideous mistakes; they commit frightful wrongs; they do great and beautiful things. And shall we not best guide humanity by telling the truth about all this, so far as the truth is ascertainable?[7]

Even more than in Du Bois's time, states today have shown themselves to be a threat to a planet in crisis, yet they and their rulers are redeemed by the religiosity of many authoritarian leftists. As Anto-

[7] W. E. B. Du Bois, *Black Reconstruction in America* (New York: Free Press, 1998), 714.

nio Gramsci noted, "The historical unity of the ruling classes is realized in the state, and their history is essentially the history of states and groups of states."[8] States require ruling classes and vice versa, and the revolutionary past of a country like the Soviet Union, when it existed, didn't change this fact. C. L. R. James, who lived through the era of the Russian Revolution and a global left dominated by Stalinism, understood this well. In a collaboration with Raya Dunayevskaya and Grace Lee Boggs, James criticized both Stalinism and Trotskyism in *State Capitalism and World Revolution*, writing that their approaches were held back by their authoritarianism and limited analysis. Moreover, James maintained that the "revolutionary" state, with its new ruling class, had not even overthrown capital: "The plan, the party, the state are totally capitalistic. Nazi or Stalinist, they represent capital."[9]

When state-building (or state-justification) becomes the priority of authoritarian leftists, the state and its prisons, military, and other forms of violence become conflated with revolution itself and, from there, with "the people." This way the state doesn't supposedly represent the people, it *becomes* the people. C. L. R. James makes a similar point in *Facing Reality*:

[8] Antonio Gramsci, *Selections from the Prison Notebooks*, edited by Quinton Hoare and Geoffrey Nowell Smith (New York: International Publishers, 1971), 52.

[9] C. L. R. James, Raya Dunayevskaya, and Grace Lee Boggs, *State Capitalism and World Revolution* (Oakland: PM Press, 2013), 57.

The whole world today lives in the shadow of state power. This state power is an ever-present self-perpetuating body over and above society. It transforms the human personality into a mass of economic needs to be satisfied by decimal points of economic progress. It robs everyone of initiative and clogs the free development of society. This state power, by whatever name it is called, One-Party state or Welfare state, destroys all pretense of government by the people, of the people. All that remains is government for the people.[10]

James compares Hitler and Stalin repeatedly, showing the parallels between different forms of state authority. He notes how they both went about erasing people's autonomy in order to become "the sole individuals in their countries entitled to any personality at all." At the same time, he notes that "political parties in parliamentary democracies become machines in which the individual must either conform or be ruthlessly eliminated. Human associations no longer are guided by leadership, they pay homage to 'the leader.'" These problems are not limited to one type of state. "There is not a single national concentration of power and privilege in official society which would not mutilate and torture its own population in the Hitler-Stalin manner if it needed to, and could."[11] When a state's

[10] C. L. R. James, Grace Lee Boggs, and Cornelius Castoriadus, *Facing Reality* (Chicago: Charles H. Kerr, 2006), 9.

[11] Ibid., 69, 73, 80.

actions are the people's actions, any group of rulers can be absorbed by its infallible body and claim to act in the people's interests while maintaining state power as a weapon used to crush populations. The *actual* people are left defenseless while state apparatuses protect themselves.

In a process that mirrors that of other forms of celebrity, revolutionary leaders are those who have "made it" or "won." In this, they share important features with the leaders of less blatantly authoritarian liberal democracies, with their systems of representation, parties, and electability. States are states, and those who aspire to run them are rulers. The belief that any state that opposes the United States must therefore be good is a fallacy that is incredibly dangerous. Capitalism is global, and states submit to the will of the global market. This requires forms of oppression, exploitation, and inequality that, while the details may vary, are inherent in the state form. While they may not admit it, and may not fully understand it themselves, authoritarian leftists in the United States don't necessarily want to abolish prisons, police, or militaries in the same way other leftists do. They may want to change their form, but since they support other states that use the same structures it is clear that they simply want them overseen by leaders they admire.

This reduces revolutionary politics to mere jostling for power, which doesn't defeat the likes of state capitalism or fascist threats. Lorenzo Kom'boa Ervin suggested tactically separating from

Marxist-Leninists through "studies of the authoritarian personality to help us organize against fascist recruitment." According to Ervin:

All the M-L's "United Fronts" care about is a strict political approach to defeat fascism and prevent them from attaining state power, while being able to usher the Communist party in instead. They organize liberals and others into mass coalitions just to seize power, and then crush all radical and liberal ideological opponents after they get done with the fascists. That is why the Stalinist "Communist" states resemble fascist police states so much in refusing to allow ideological plurality—they are both totalitarian. For that matter, how much difference was there really between Stalin and Hitler? So, I say that merely physically beating back the fascists is not the issue. We need to study what accounts for the mass psychology of fascism and then defeat it ideologically, going to the core of the deep-seated racist beliefs, emotions, and authoritarian conditioning of those workers who support fascism and all police state authority.[12]

Relatedly, throughout his work Ervin also urges leftists to reject vanguardism, one of many issues he lists as hindering revolution. It clashes with the left's need for voluntary and participatory associations by assuming people need to be led by an established vanguard party. This assumption is shared by far too many on the left, and,

[12] Lorenzo Kom'boa Ervin, *Anarchism and the Black Revolution*, theanar chistlibrary.org/library/lorenzo-kom-boa-ervin-anarchism-and-the-black-revolution.

though Ervin's critique is largely directed at the white left, it happens beyond it too. Left vanguards can be playgrounds for egos, places where competition and self-aggrandizement provide cover for the logics of capitalism and white supremacy. The things I've discussed all contribute to the lack of a mass movement of the left that is truly a threat to capitalism or the state. All the fault does not lie with the authoritarian leftists, though. Classical anarchist traditions—that is, European and predominantly white anarchism—have largely been critical of many of the problems I've mentioned. However, within the United States and Europe they have failed to properly appeal to and struggle with masses of people who are not white. The distinct Black anarchistic and autonomous politics that I use to think through the problems above provide an important shift in emphasis. They arose out of a need to focus on the problems of Black people that white anarchists were not addressing. The result is sets of politics that avoid many of the pitfalls of the authoritarian *and* classical anarchist left but also point us toward solutions applicable to the entire left.

There's no agreed upon narrative about what Black anarchism is or when and where it began. However, one prominent understanding sees it as a development within as well as a breaking away from organizations of the Black liberation movements of the 1960s and 1970s, especially the civil rights and Black Power movements. People who took part in these movements began to see limitations in their approaches. Aside from Ervin, some other early and influential Black anarchists are Ashanti Alston, Kuwasi Balagoon, Martin Sostre, and Ojore Lutalo. These were revolutionaries who became disillusioned with things they saw happening in the Black Panther Party and Black movements they had been participating in. As Lutalo describes it: "In 1975 I became disillusioned with Marxism and became an anarchist (thanks to Kuwasi Balagoon) due to the inactiveness and ineffectiveness of Marxism in our communities along with repressive bureaucracy that comes with Marxism."[13] So they turned away from Leninism, Stalinism, and Maoism toward the development of Black and New Afrikan anarchisms. This is something that distinguishes Black anarchism from classical anarchism. It is a split from within Black movements as opposed to simply being an effort to diversify or revise classical anarchism. White anarchists and others who herald the latter and defend the whiteness of anarchist movements by tokenizing Black anarchists highlight another dogmatic misstep. Black anarchism, of course, has much in common with classical anarchism, but it is Black-centered, specific to Black people and our unique conditions. The challenge it represents parallels developments within what Cedric Robinson calls the "Black radical tradition," which recognizes and addresses the "conflicts extant between Western radicalism and the struggle for Black libera-

[13] "Ojore Lutalo," Anarchist Black Cross Federation website, www.abcf.net/prisoners/lutalo.htm.

tion."[14] In the past, Black radicals have broken with and confronted Marxism. Black anarchism does this with Marxism, certain Black mass movements, and classical anarchism. It transcends the left as we know it, and its existence in and of itself represents a failure of the anarchist movement.

Furthermore, classical anarchists have what often feels like a problem of perpetual reactivity. Like the authoritarian left, they have developed their own fixed narratives about themselves, filled with heroes and, especially, martyrs. They have their luminaries— Bakunin, Kropotkin, Goldman, and others—and find it hard to move beyond them. Historically, anarchist movements have suffered very real harms and traumas, often at the hands of authoritarian socialists and the states they founded. Because of this historical trauma, they find it incredibly difficult to move beyond the harm experienced in the past. They embrace a historical narrative of abuse and injury and become lost in reactive cycles that fracture any proactive revolutionary impulse. We can return again to Cedric Robinson:

Anarchy is . . . like a sparrow which once wounded never flies again. Its injuries are attended to, its feathers grown out and put in order, but the critical psychological, instinctual trauma is never healed.

[14] Cedric J. Robinson, *Black Marxism: The Making of the Black Radical Tradition* (Chapel Hill: University of North Carolina Press, 2000), 308.

The anarchists were reflex to an evil history which penetrated their own remarkable and macabre achievements. In their efforts, the state was countered by the dissolution of the state, centralization by decentralization, elitist intellectualism by pedestrian peasantism, force by reason, obedience by disobedience, familiar entropy by ordered familiarity. They had failed to free themselves, to disengage meaningfully from the existential boundaries and force of their own experience. They were (and are) forever in the state clawing out to a thing perceived through the eyes of naive, desperate infancy.

Anarchism was a theory of society conscious of and in opposition to political society. Though anarchist theorists attempted to reconstruct social order mainly on the basis of economic authority, their conceptualizations of social order had identical epistemological and metaphysical foundations to that which they sought to oppose.[15]

Internal critique and self-reflection are important to any social movement or political grouping, and anarchism is no exception. In this regard, I have learned a lot from Buddhist teachings, especially Zen Buddhism, which questions institutional rigidity and unthinking reactiveness. The person alleged to have brought proto-Zen teachings from India to China was the monk Bodhidharma. Writings attributed to or about him and the circle of disciples he gathered often provide brilliant lessons that political thinkers would do

[15] Robinson, *Terms of Order*, 185.

well to learn. In one story, a practitioner named Master Yüan resoundingly critiques dogma, scripture, and tradition. Master Yüan is asked, "Does one rely on Dharma [Buddhist doctrine or teachings] or does one rely on people?"[16] Yüan replies:

> In accordance with my understanding, you rely on neither people nor Dharma. If you rely on Dharma and do not rely on people, it is still one way of viewing things. If you rely on people and do not rely on Dharma, it is the same.... If you have bodily energy, you will avoid the deceptive delusions of people and Dharma, and your spirit will be all right. Why? Because when you esteem knowledge, you are deceived by men and Dharma. If you value one person as correct, then you will not avoid the deceptive confusions of this person, and this is true even to the point where, if you say that a Buddha is the supreme person, you will not avoid deception. Why? Because you are deluded about the realm of objects. Because, by relying on this person, your mind of faith becomes heavy.[17]

As many have noted before, Buddhist teachings often can be interpreted in ways that are relevant to anarchism, but this instance stands out in its precision. Master Yüan's critique of the overreliance on dogma and teachers speaks clearly to the melding of revolutionary thought and revolutionaries with revolution itself. In Master

[16] Jeffrey L Broughton, ed., *The Bodhidharma Anthology: The Earliest Records of Zen* (Berkeley: University of California Press, 1999), 39.

[17] Ibid.

Yüan's response, even the Buddha himself is not to be esteemed as a "supreme person." The deceptiveness of such idolatry replaces vital social movements with stagnant cults of personality. Political celebrity, even bestowed on people who have done great things, almost invariably leads to corruption and distorts our goals for collective betterment.

Nationalism and the state form itself are incarnations of this sort of institutional dogma. Capitalism and the state push ideological doctrines that function as quasi-religious tenets. Just as many conservative religious doctrines encourage people to hate themselves—as unworthy sinners, as weak and flawed and perhaps dangerous without being overseen by their gods—the state instills a self-image in people that makes them psychologically rely on it or even worship it. By seeing state dogma in this way, we can begin to understand why the state's more passionate supporters embrace its violence and oppression. What becomes perplexing, though, is that authoritarian leftists consider state forms as revolutionary alternatives. Just as some oppressed people in the United States may think that "freedom" means having what rich or famous people have, authoritarian leftists seek to build their own versions of what oppresses us, a new state-centered faith.

Leftist zealots attach themselves to dead leaders and dwell on them to the point that they become supernatural beings. Like some sort of mourning that refuses to ever pass, this turns the past into a fetish, much like "the good old days" are for conservatives. Conservatives, at least, are consistent: they don't want change. On the left, this sort of behavior is especially hypocritical. This constipated revolutionary mourning can be surpassed if we can learn to let go and *live* the ideals that we currently idolize and fossilize. And it's important to admit that our predecessors and ancestors themselves may not have embodied these ideals as well as we imagine in our romantic revisioning of them. No one is above critique, and not everyone who claimed to hate the state, empire, and oppression actually did. "If you meet a buddha," says Zen master Lin-Chi, "kill the buddha."[18]

In his work, *Hammer and Hoe*, Robin D. G. Kelley describes the struggle of communists in the 1930s and 1940s in Alabama. He details how some Black communists imagined a new war might bring about the needed change they hoped for to liberate them from the miserable conditions of the racist apartheid South. "What distinguished this 'new war' from the Civil War and Reconstruction was its international dimension. For many black radicals the Russians were the 'new Yankees,' Stalin was the 'new Lincoln,' and the Soviet Union was a 'new Ethiopia' stretching forth her arms in defense of black folk. Southern propaganda depicting Communists as 'Soviet

[18] Burton Watson, ed., *The Zen Teachings of Master Lin-Chi* (New York: Columbia University Press, 1999), 52.

agents' worked to the Party's advantage in black working-class communities. The idea of Soviet and/or Northern radical support provided a degree of psychological confidence for African-Americans hoping to wage the long-awaited revolution in the South."[19]

Ultimately, Kelley describes something similar to the problem I'm addressing on the left. He notes, "Faced with the centrality of Russia in popular notions of Communism, black radicals (unconsciously) constructed a folklore that mythologized the Soviet Union."[20] This sort of thinking underpins the history of Black anarchism because the leadership of the Black Panther Party adopted models based on state-socialist leaders and centralization. This led to disillusionment and frustration among those who would eventually break away in favor of Black anarchism. Black Panther field marshal Don Cox recalls some of his frustrations in his memoir:

> The major weakness—one that inevitably leads to failure—is Lenin's idea that a party should be structured according to the tenets of democratic centralism. Under utopian conditions, with everyone being more or less an angel, it would probably work; but given our present stage of evolutionary development, with all our human strengths and weaknesses, it is just not possible to pull it off. Lenin either gave no con-

[19] Robin D. G. Kelley, *Hammer and Hoe: Alabama Communists during the Great Depression* (Chapel Hill: University of North Carolina Press, 2015), 100.
[20] Ibid.

sideration to, or ignored the fact, that whenever a member of the human species gets into a position to exercise power, something goes haywire. Since all intellectual activity is subjective, those exercising power —defined as the ability to use resources, whether human or otherwise, to act upon the environment to bring about change—do so in their own subjective ways. The degree of benefit to the masses is dependent upon the coincidence of the subjective ideas of those exercising power and the real needs of the people.

Given the present state of our social development, in which power is often centered on small groups, we must be extremely vigilant. Progressive organizations that presume to move in the interest of the masses must constantly confront the psychology of power. In some form or fashion, they must devise checks and balances to control the madness that seems to arise whenever power is concentrated in the hands of a few individuals. Democratic centralism is not the answer. It is the mechanism that gave us Stalin and Hilliard. Inevitably, when this form of organizational structure is adopted, centralism is emphasized, often to the detriment of democracy, and that leads to authoritarianism, to bureaucracy, and to dictatorship.[21]

Clearly this problem is not only one of the past; it's one that has persisted through changing political climates and circumstances.

[21] Don Cox, *Just Another Nigger: My Life in the Black Panther Party* (Berkeley: Heyday, 2019), 205.

Black people have faced a climate of repression almost impossible to imagine. It's gone on long enough for us to challenge the notion that we should be waiting for *any* state or leader to liberate us. Idealizing states, ideologues, revolutionaries, and cultish leadership models falls short of encouraging the development of transformative politics.

It's very hard to get these points across. One of the major problems with leftist zealots is that, like any zealots, the more you tell them that they're being illogical, the more they think they're right and that your resistance is evidence of counterrevolutionary deviation. Since their worldview revolves around a romanticization of being alienated for their perceived correctness, they often embrace criticism as a sign that they're correct. They are so dogmatic that they are obsessed with punishing and disciplining people who do not meet their standards for political purity. So, when you levy critique against them, they seek to banish, shun, or exile you. The organizing we need to do and the political education necessary to do it must overcome this sort of desperate adherence to models and political approaches that haven't gotten us where we need to be.

New Afrikan anarchist Kuwasi Balagoon raised many of these issues, though in a global context. However, he made sure to keep a realistic perspective about the complexity of different struggles. We should consider what he said in this regard. "The only way to make a dictatorship of the proletariat is to elevate everyone to being pro-letariat and deflate all the advantages of power that translate into the wills of a few dictating to the majority. The possibility must be prevented of any individual or group of individuals being able to en-force their wills over any other individual's private life or to extract social consequences for behavior preferences or ideas."[22] He goes on, though, to clarify that this means granting people the right to choose their own forms of rebellion:

> It is beside the point whether Black, Puerto Rican, Native American and Chicano- Mexicano people endorse nationalism as a vehicle for self-de-termination or agree with anarchism as being the only road to self-de-termination. As revolutionaries we must support the will of the masses. It is not only racism but compliance with the enemy to stand outside of the social arena and permit America to continue to practice genocide against the Third World captive colonies because although they resist, they don't agree with us. If we truly know that Anarchy is the best way of life for all people, we must promote it, defend it and know that the people who are as smart as we are will accept it.[23]

[22] Kuwasi Balagoon, "Anarchy Can't Fight Alone," in *A Soldier's Story: Revolutionary Writings by a New Afrikan Anarchist* (Oakland: PM Press, 2019), 151–52.

[23] Ibid., 153.

The self-explanatory title of the Balagoon essay quoted here is "Anarchy Can't Fight Alone." However, it should not be assumed that the soundness of anarchists challenging the necessity of states, nationalism, and (usually) cults of personality lets them off the hook. The failures of anarchist movements to have a wider appeal and, in the United States, the tendency for the anarchist movement to be seen as white, utopian, individualistic, and quasi-liberal should be both critiqued and addressed. Balagoon makes this much clear:

> Our inactivity creates a void that this police state, with its reactionary press and definite goals, is filling. The parts of people's lives supposedly touched by mass organizing and revolutionary inspiration that sheds a light that encourages them to unveil a new day, instead are being manipulated by conditions of which apathy is no less a part than poisonous uncontested reactionary propaganda. To those who believe in a centralized party with a program for the masses this might mean whatever their subjective analysis permits. But to us who truly believe in the masses and believe that they should have their lives in their hands and know that freedom is a habit, this can only mean that we have far to go.[24]

The distance between the left as it currently exists and the left as we need it to be is too great to hesitate any longer. I am not a sectarian. I understand politics based on what I feel makes most sense

[24] Ibid., 152–53.

from the ideologies, philosophies, and traditions I know. We can shape our politics based on how various theories and analyses do or do not work for us here and now. In whatever conditions we face, praxis defines the worth of our ideas. The goal of liberation may be one of the few things we share. What that looks like and how we get there is always capable of changing. However, worship, proselytizing, or semi-religious attempts at conversion are not likely to be useful approaches. The same is true of elevating people to the status of revered leaders. Those who we learn from are not the final answer themselves but rather stepping-stones toward clarity on these matters. The truth itself is supreme, not those who lead us closer to it by purpose, chance, or coincidence.

A functioning, organized opposition will not be a bunch of bickering factions who sacrifice accomplishment for the sake of their social clubs and cliques. It will require large numbers of different people coming together with their own unique perspectives, talents, and smarts to upend what we agree should no longer stand. Many of us have more in common than we may want to admit, but one of the most important things we share is a threat. This isn't something to take lightly. State violence is real and deadly. We are largely unprepared and disorganized. We need to find and join together with those who are ready for abolition, the dismantling of oppressive power in all its forms. We must abandon fantasies that point us toward failed methods and fruitless directions. Things that do not do the work of building revolutionary abolitionist efforts and that favor reformism should be left behind. We should study foundational thought and major contributions, understanding that a variety of thinkers may have something to offer and that they all are worthy of critique. The moment we become more committed to sect than we are to liberation, we have betrayed ourselves. To be free, we have to be prepared to discard ideas that are not bringing about freedom.

There can be great benefit in cooperation around common goals, but that doesn't mean those of us who want liberation should accept *any* absurd or violent political visions. It is okay to struggle with respect for those who differ from us *and* to denounce irresponsible calls for unity. There is no label, identity, or set of politics that is essential to understanding and undertaking what needs to be done. Black anarchism has been useful in framing much of my thinking, but as an ideology or doctrine it is not the goal. We need action, and rejecting fantasy gives us a better sense of the reality within which we must act. It's not hard to see what is coming, what is already here. Black anarchism can help us to understand how history is twisted and misused, so that we can better face what's ahead.

CHAPTER FOUR

THE GREAT RETURN

*You can't name where I ain't been down, 'cause there
ain't no place I ain't been down.* —Gil Scott Heron

Since the past shapes our perception of the world around us, seeing
the continuum helps us as we encounter everything that's wrong
now. When we critically examine the narratives we've internalized,
we're better equipped for the troubling present day. There are
predicaments in front of us related to movement, environment, and
the state that demand an unflinching, radical honesty in this regard.
We cannot deceive ourselves about where we're coming from in order to get where we need to go. And it's the act of going or moving
that I hope to address here.

The question of Black citizenship is intricately linked to the
struggle of migrants, immigrants, refugees, the undocumented, and
other precarious classifications. In the United States, migration is
usually associated with people from South and Central America living in the United States, particularly those who are not Black. Common perceptions of immigration have excluded Black people for a

number of reasons. Among those is the fact that Black people are discriminated against even in immigrant rights movements. We are erased from migrant and immigrant narratives much like we're erased from the citizen category.

Black family histories contain many stories of kin fleeing the South to avoid the terror of white violence. The Great Migration, as we know it, the endless movement of Black Americans around the country seeking jobs, safety, and other resources, is something Black anarchism can diagnose as an important aspect of our struggle. Black people had to shed fears of borders, challenge ideas of place, and practice mutual aid to survive unknown landscapes. Zora Neale Hurston offers a relevant portrait of the Black migrant in *Their Eyes Were Watching God*:

> Day by day now, the hordes of workers poured in. Some came limping in with their shoes and sore feet from walking. It's hard trying to follow your shoe instead of your shoe following you. They came in wagons from way up in Georgia and they came in truck loads from east, west, north and south. Permanent transients with no attachments and tired looking men with their families and dogs in flivvers. All night, all day, hurrying in to pick beans. Skillets, beds, patched up spare inner tubes all hanging and dangling from the ancient cars on the outside and hopeful humanity, herded and hovered on the inside, chugging on to the muck. People ugly from ignorance and broken from being poor.

All night now the jooks clanged and clamored. Pianos living three lifetimes in one. Blues made and used right on the spot. Dancing, fighting, singing, crying, laughing, winning and losing love every hour. Work all day for money, fight all night for love. The rich black earth clinging to bodies and biting the skin like ants.[1]

Black migrants were working to meet the demands of a capitalist country that did not consider them actual citizens. People traveled and fled, like they do now, because they had no choice. Their goals and hopes for themselves *required* movement. This consistently involuntary movement has rarely been seen as a migration struggle. Black people and our constant relocations are being erased from dominant narratives in the United States, rendering us neither citizen nor noncitizen, highlighting alienation and perpetual displacement under both classifications. Significantly, this is continuing under the violence we know as "gentrification." Black people are being displaced, upended, and expelled from places we've long known as home. Many of us are being forced to find new places that are more affordable and reasonable in order to build safe and happy lives. In this context, it's important that we recall the Black histories of movement and build solidarity with those being forced to move across the diaspora.

[1] Zora Neale Hurston, *Their Eyes Were Watching God* (New York: Harper Collins, 2004), 131.

Forced relocation defines Black existence across the Americas. There is a direct line from Black people being forced onto plantations as property to today's experiences of being unsettled and repeatedly relocated. Africans being transported for the purposes of slavery entered the United States through the Old South before the country began its rapid, violent expansion. A large forced migration of Black people happened between the Old South (Virginia, the Carolinas, Georgia) and the New South based on the shifting demands of agriculture, new crops, and labor. Black movement to California between 1850 and 1860 established the first English-speaking Black communities out west and marked another significant movement (forced and otherwise) of Black people.[2]

Following the Civil War and "emancipation," Black people trying to make a life in the period of Reconstruction were met with heinous violence. As W. E. B. Du Bois writes in *Black Reconstruction*, "The result of the war left four million human beings just as valuable for the production of cotton and sugar as they had been before the war."[3] White supremacy, unbroken by war but perturbed

[2] The first Black people in present-day Los Angeles were from Mexico. These early Angelenos of African descent made up a significant portion of the city's founders.

[3] W. E. B. Du Bois, *Black Reconstruction in America* (New York: Free Press, 1998), 238.

and resentful in the South, exercised vengeance on the lives of Black people trying to survive as best they knew how. It reformed itself through updated imprisoning mechanisms and violent authoritarian surveillance and policing that we still live with today. The trauma brought on by ceaseless white terror was the only inheritance many were promised for their grueling labor. So, many had to flee the South.

What is popularly known as the Great Migration took place between the early twentieth century and the 1970s. However, we'd do well to understand it never truly stopped. This movement of Black migrants hoping to find better lives free from oppression and economic exploitation transformed the country. Documenting her own family history and movement, Christina Sharpe explains that relocation is not exclusive to Black people in the United States nor did it satisfy hopes for freedom:

> This, of course, is not wholly, or even largely, a Black US phenomenon. This kind of movement happens all over the Black diaspora from and in the Caribbean and the continent to the metropole, the US great migrations of the early to mid-twentieth century that saw millions of Black people moving from the South to the North, and those people on the move in the contemporary from points all over the African continent to other points on the continent and also to Germany, Greece,

Lampedusa. Like many of these Black people on the move, my parents discovered that things were not better in this "new world": the subjections of constant and overt racism and isolation continued.[4]

That hope for a better life, however marred by the reality of Black existence, has everything to do with what we're experiencing today. Black people's lives regularly face disruption around the planet, no matter where we're located. Within the U.S. borders, this means moving around domestically, while Black people from outside the country regularly try to enter; both are seeking safety and stability. As we move around within and between nations, crossing borders, hoping to secure a home, we're bound to exclusion based on our history. Creating our own false narratives has not granted us true inclusion in categories like citizenship or provided any sort of liberation. Tales of being selfless patriots who made America great, just like tales of being descendants of kings and queens, have not overcome this. Nor has any self-aggrandizing revolutionary leftist ideology.

Black people are kept outside the categories that other people see as basic rights. Nations and societies declare us unfit, undeserving, and unaccepted. The violence historically levied against us extends to forcible displacement from our homes and our roots. Black

---

[4] Christina Elizabeth Sharpe, *In the Wake: On Blackness and Being* (Durham, NC: Duke University Press, 2016), 4.

people in the United States and throughout the world experience the extraordinary brutality of being people with no place on the map. And many of the paths people look to for liberation offer us nothing.

In the United States, being treated as a necessary sacrifice for the sake of the nation-state complicates this further. The violence against us is made into something that's immutable but also part of a narrative of national progress. Our struggles historically, from enslavement to Jim Crow to now, have been embraced by the state under banners of memorial and commemoration. Yet something more sinister happens here when museums, schools, and institutes dedicated to the preservation of Black history make that very history into something that the country needed to become what it is now. This assumes, of course, that today is satisfactory and that our struggle is finished or nearly concluded. All the displacement, brutality, and murder are seen as beneficial for the sake of social change. The United States is then a complete, finalized democracy thanks to Black suffering that gains temporary reforms that supposedly prove the state's good intentions. In reality, those reforms have often been ploys to avoid further uprisings and maintain oppression. At times, some segments of Black mass movements have embraced the messaging and narratives of national progress. Pan-African social ecologist Modibo Kadalie has offered criticism in this regard stating, "The civil rights and Black power movements were based upon the

Waiting to move at Five Points MARTA stop

inaccurate premise that we were struggling to force America to live up to the true meaning of its creed. America has always lived up to the true meaning of its creed. Its creed is genocide and slavery."[5] All of these distortions of history reinforce the idea that this country is somewhere migrants, immigrants, and refugees can find freedom, despite the fact that Black migrants have been attempting to do this by moving around within its boundaries for centuries.

Abroad, migrants, immigrants, and refugees make their way to the gates of other countries and are denied entry. The Global South is also sacrificed for the betterment and comfort of states that feed on exploited communities within the so-called third world. The rampant and unrelenting exploitation of and extraction from the Global South forces millions into movement fleeing the violence of empire. And this theft of wealth requires political and military control. The Guyanese revolutionary Walter Rodney speaks to this with regard to the African continent, although it applies similarly elsewhere: "If economic power is centered outside national African boundaries, then political and military power in any real sense is also centered outside until, and unless, the masses of peasants and workers are mobilized to offer an alternative to the system of sham polit-

[5] Modibo Kadalie, *Pan-African Social Ecology: Speeches, Conversations, and Essays* (Atlanta: On Our Own Authority!, 2019), 69.

ical independence. All of those features are ramifications of under-development and of the exploitation of the imperialist system."[6]

Countless coups, interventions, and wars have shaken the stability of communities around the world. Since the imperialists cannot steal and extract without control, they maintain their influence in the governing bodies of the states they seek to exploit. People or governments that pose a threat must be overthrown, sabotaged, and undermined. When you control as much capital and have the influence that the West does, this comes with ease. However, this isn't limited to states that are a part of the West. Plenty of states exploit internationally and oppress vulnerable populations within their borders. States that have had less opportunity to do so are not automatically revolutionary because of that fact, nor are they because they espouse revolutionary values or histories while adhering to the rules of "the free market." All of it still forces people to move and suffer the instabilities of displacement.

The people being forced to leave their homes around the world that are a part of the African diaspora pay the price of empire and state violence. People leave the African continent and experience terrifying voyages by boat and otherwise, trying to reach Europe, a region that has, through extraction and plunder, created the intol-

[6] Walter Rodney, *How Europe Underdeveloped Africa* (London: Verso Books, 2018), 33.

erable conditions they are fleeing. While the meddling exploitation of states destabilizes, people die in great numbers just trying to survive inside and outside of borders. This forced movement, all of these deaths in the mountains, oceans, seas, and deserts, are not simply news stories that don't concern us. We are connected to them not just because we're Black people but also because our respective pasts and oppressed existences share commonalities. These shared understandings of how we're being exploited are what we need to build from in order to create a global push for a revolutionary uprising. Our continual, global displacement forces our movement in this sense as well.

In the United States, Black people are constantly being cycled around the country by the whims of capital. Gentrification is pushing families and entire communities to the brink, displacing people who have never known anything but the place they're being forced to leave. And much like the people abroad being forced to leave their home countries, those forcing Black people out here only see opportunity and profit. The Great Migration that dispersed Black America is being reversed, and new paths are being traveled by poor and working-class people who can't afford to stay where they are. Black people are moving all around *again*, many returning to the South. These are the circumstances under which we must organize, abolishing the conditions that force us into movement and establishing networks of communities that will become the society we need.

Since abolition requires us to create the future we desire through undoing, now is of the utmost importance.

In 1943, Zora Neale Hurston documented in "The 'Pet Negro' System" how the South was marked by its racist reputation, writing, "It has been so generally accepted that all Negroes in the South are living under horrible conditions that many friends of the Negro up North actually take offense if you don't tell them a tale of horror and suffering."[7] She describes a narrative that still persists today among many, including Black people who fear ever living in a conservative stronghold. Just as generations of Black people earlier sought respite from southern apartheid in the North and West and found little if any, Black people returning to the South are finding gentrification and other oppressive circumstances. As Malcolm X once told us, "If you are Black, you were born in jail, in the North as well as the South."[8] One thing is certain, there is no safety within the boundaries of empire, but perhaps safe havens may be found in its abolition. Traveling for extended periods of time makes one so worn and weary. We deserve more than a pit stop; we deserve a safe home. What home means has to take our current reality into serious consideration. The words of the poet Dionne Brand can guide us well here:

[7] Zora Neale Hurston, "The 'Pet Negro' System," *American Mercury*, May 1943, 593–600.

[8] Malcolm X, "Black Nationalism Can Set Us Free," n.d., audio recording, www.marxists.org/reference/archive/malcolm-x/index.htm.

Canadians and Americans who police these fresh borders, materially as well as intellectually, play and dwell in the same language of their conquest. A language which summons mystery and wilderness. . . . Some of us want entry into the home and nation that are signified by these romances. Some of us in the Diaspora long so for nation—some continuous thread of biological or communal association, some blood-line or legacy which will cement our rights in the place we live. The problem of course is that even if those existed—and they certainly do, even if it is in the human contraband which we represent in the romance—they do not guarantee nation for Blacks in the Diaspora.[9]

As Zoé Samudzi and I explained in *As Black as Resistance*, it's important that we not try to establish *anything* "on top of centuries-old exterminatory settler logic of Indigenous removal and geno-cide."[10] Land and liberation must go beyond the idea that the nation-state is a crucial precursor to actualize liberation. State-building has had plenty of opportunities to show us all of its danger-ous risks and problems, and we should not reproduce the systems of exclusion that have never accepted us. Thus, I'm certainly not ar-guing for inclusion in the current "our" that people speak of when they say "our nation." Nor do I think we should create a new

[9] Dionne Brand, *A Map to the Door of No Return: Notes to Belonging* (Toronto: Vintage Canada, 2001), 67.

[10] Zoé Samudzi and William C. Anderson, *As Black as Resistance: Finding the Conditions for Liberation* (Oakland: AK Press, 2018), 31.

"our"—as in "our nation," "our military," "our prisons," and so on. Mine is a call to dissolve and abolish these ideas within ourselves and around us. This can take us much further than trying to reshape horrible institutions for our own purposes.

Under conditions Black people experience, the idea of creating liberated zones comes to the forefront of many people's minds. In various revolutionary traditions in the past, this has meant attempting to build "the commune."

The commune hasn't just been a whimsical, utopian idea: it's been a necessity for Black people seeking something different. The commune, the federation (i.e., the network of free communes), and collective land "ownership" are ideas and practices that have long existed, but they need to be more extensively understood. Referencing Huey P. Newton, prison activist and Black revolutionary George Jackson described the commune as "the central city-wide revolutionary culture" that will pose "a significant challenge to property rights."[11] He went further to provide specific detail and instruction about how to claim rights as our own that have not been respected, such as property rights:

> It will involve building a political, social and economic infrastructure, capable of filling the vacuum that has been left by the establishment

[11] George Jackson, *Blood in My Eye* (Baltimore: Black Classic Press, 1990), 123.

ruling class and pushing the occupying forces of the enemy culture from our midst. The implementation of this new social, political and economic program will feed and comfort all the people on at least a subsistence level, and force the "owners" of the enemy bourgeois culture either to tie their whole fortunes to the communes and the people, or to leave the land, the tools and the market behind.[12]

There are important distinctions we should examine that separate what I am describing from certain forms of nationalism and from the false freedom and illusory autonomy of "Black capitalism." Black anarchists have taken this in their own direction, rejecting the worn-out practices of vanguardism and state-building when it comes to the commune. For example, Lorenzo Kom'boa Ervin, referencing Jackson's ideas, explains the commune in this way:

The idea behind a mass commune is to create a dual power structure as a counter to the government, under conditions which exist now. In fact, Anarchists believe the first step toward self-determination and the Social revolution is Black control of the Black community. This means that Black people must form and unify their own organizations of struggle, take control of the existing Black communities and all the institutions within them, and conduct a consistent fight to overcome every form of economic, political and cultural servitude, and any system of

[12] Ibid., 123–24.

racial and class inequality which is the product of this racist Capitalist society.... The Commune is also a Black revolutionary counterculture. It is the embryo of the new Black revolutionary society in the body of the old sick, dying one. It is the new lifestyle in microcosm, which contains the new Black social values and the new communal organizations, and institutions, which will become the sociopolitical infrastructure of the free society.[13]

Kuwasi Balagoon approaches the commune in his own way, although he also calls for efforts that would rely on mass organizing and collective work. He situates the commune in the context of a larger shift, in which day-to-day interactions become more intentional and liberatory:

Where we live and work, we must not only escalate discussion and study groups, we must also organize on the ground level. The landlords must be contested through rent strikes and rather than develop strategies to pay the rent, we should develop strategies to take the buildings. We must not only recognize the squatters' movement for what it is, but support and embrace it. Set up communes in abandoned buildings, sell scrap cars and aluminum cans. Turn vacant lots into gardens. When our children grow out of clothes, we should have places where we can take

[13] Lorenzo Kom'boa Ervin, *Anarchism and the Black Revolution*, theanar chistlibrary.org/library/lorenzo-kom-boa-ervin-anarchism-and-the-black-revolution.

LaPlace, Louisiana

them, clearly marked anarchist clothing exchanges and have no bones about looking for clothing there first. And of course we should relearn how to preserve food; we must learn construction and ways to take back our lives, help each other move and stay in shape.[14]

The commune does not have to be called "the commune" or thought about in outdated ways. The important point is rejecting the everyday realities of capitalism in our day-to-day lives. This is something Black people are forced to do by the intentional neglect inflicted upon us by the state. Over a century before Zoé Samudzi and I wrote about the anarchism of Blackness, W. E. B. Du Bois posited that the alienation Black people experience could be used with radical purpose in our struggles. He famously wrote that we were "gifted with second-sight in this American world."[15] This second sight provides an ability to gain a deeper perception of the problems around us when it is properly cultivated.

Compare this with what former member of the Black Liberation Army and Anarchist Panther Ashanti Alston wrote in one of his most notable essays, *Black Anarchism*:

[14] Kuwasi Balagoon, "Anarchy Can't Fight Alone," in *A Soldier's Story: Revolutionary Writings by a New Afrikan Anarchist* (Oakland: PM Press, 2019), 154.

[15] W. E. B. Du Bois, *The Souls of Black Folk* (1904; repr., New York: Barnes & Noble Classics, 2003), 9.

I think of being Black not so much as an ethnic category but as an oppositional force or touchstone for looking at situations differently. Black culture has always been oppositional and is all about finding ways to creatively resist oppression here, in the most racist country in the world. So, when I speak of a Black anarchism, it is not so tied to the color of my skin but who I am as a person, as someone who can resist, who can see differently when I am stuck, and thus live differently.[16]

We are not supernatural beings or inherently political, but there is so much potential among us. Understanding this can spark the fires of confrontation with our past, our present, and our future. It can help us identify, challenge, and discard the leftism that is not serving us, as well as give us a clear picture of our relationship to the state. Our experience tells us that our commune must be stateless. We are different Black people from different places across the country arriving at similar conclusions over a great span of time. This is no accident, but where are we going with it and how will our lived knowledge make our lives better?

Facing precarious conditions, Black people have worked tirelessly to build strong communities despite the onslaught of state violence at every turn. Generations have struggled to build their own institutions within a white society—while, of course, many others

[16] Ashanti Alston, "Black Anarchism," *Perspectives on Anarchist Theory*, Spring 2004, 7–8 (transcript of talk given at Hunter College on October 24, 2003).

worked to integrate above all else. However, we cannot afford to limit ourselves in terms of how far-reaching and expansive our projects are. The "dual power"—a term tracing its origins back to Vladimir Lenin—that Ervin mentions becomes relevant here as a tool for making the state increasingly obsolete by countering it through this building process. It is, of course, only one way of describing what's needed. Some of the autonomous thinkers I'm drawing from may not favor the term or the exact idea behind it, but the core truth in its Black anarchist version is that we will have to struggle at length in order to counter the domination ruling over us. Wherever we go, we have to build, but, if that building is increasingly politicized and structured against the state, the process will hopefully lead to revolutionary abolition.

Black people have long taken whatever chances necessary to create communities that didn't resemble the oppressive circumstances we've been forced into. An important characteristic of immigrant communities moving to a new place is creating community networks that help new arrivals. Those who have gotten more adjusted and established often provide an infrastructure and even a safety net of sorts for those who come next. This is how communities grow, based on association, intimacy, and interpersonal relationships. We've always done this within the borders of the United States. As we are being forced to leave our homes around the country and seek new homes elsewhere, we clearly need the support and respite that such practices offer. How can we learn from our history of forced movement in order to create something much better?

Building toward collective sharing and radically reimagining our communities is a crucial part of our struggle. What will happen to the Black family leaving New York for Atlanta? What will the Black person fleeing Los Angeles for Houston find waiting for them when they arrive? Aside from a hope for affordable living, we should hope to work toward establishing something much more liberatory than the persistent debt and instability far too many of us know. Not only do our lives depend on it, so does the environment around us and our relation to it.

Modibo Kadalie has discussed the relation between direct democracy and our ecological emergency. He mentions what happened after the Land Act passed on the Caribbean island of Barbuda in 2007. The Land Act codified a culture of communal land ownership dating back to emancipation, but Barbudans are still fighting for their autonomy and resisting "modern-day enclosures."[17] The act was supposed to limit major development on the island by requiring the majority of residents to be in favor of it. However, following the devastation of Hurricane Irma, this ecologically conscious arrangement came under attack. Ninety percent of the island was decimated by the hurricane, and capitalists (with the help of the

[17] Kadalie, *Pan-African Social Ecology*, 133.

government) saw opportunity for development and sought to profit from the devastation. Still, Kadalie points to this example and others like the Ogeechee Rebellion and Guyana's Post-Emancipation Village movement as guides for us to understand what resistance might look like amid catastrophe. He reminds us that the state will not serve us: "It seems that almost invariably, whenever ecological crises spring up, a social vacuum is revealed and state power is unable to satisfactorily respond to these increasingly frequent and more intense catastrophes. Upon these occasions, if we look, we will find instances of direct democracy in action, however temporary or weak. We must learn to recognize, support, and strengthen them."[18]

Kadalie puts forth a much-needed call for autonomy rooted in direct democracy. He draws from C. L. R. James's *Every Cook Can Govern* among his many other works. Escalating crises are warning us we need to abolish and move beyond the state by developing ourselves and our communities into its formidable foes. There is nowhere we can run to escape oppression within the deadly borders of the state; however, we can fight to take the life of this monster no matter where we stand.

This is much bigger than us living and existing more ethically. It's about building communities that *actively* challenge capital and the

[18] Ibid., 132.

state every single day. Many among us today are already growing our own food, homeschooling, ready to defend ourselves, and practicing compassion in ways that resist capitalist ideas about how to structure daily life. Though they may not call themselves "anarchists" or "anticapitalists," the way we choose to live our lives doesn't always demand a label. The action behind it can remain just as effective without it.

We do need a conscious intention to undermine and overturn the processes that oppress us. Lorenzo Kom'boa Ervin has described such ways of building Black autonomy as simply a way to make ourselves *ungovernable*. Building functional collective structures to accomplish this requires the same gradual process as any attempt to end what's not working for us. I cannot stress enough that Black people are *already* doing all of this, but it's time to connect efforts and do this in an organized way in order to spread these practices as far as we can across the empire with explicitly politicized intentions.

It will be important to actualize this within Black migration struggles taking place around us. Black anarchism and radical Black autonomous politics prioritize collective ways of thinking and being that generate communities that push against oppressive governance —that strive to end it, not gain control over it. The great return to places we've often known through ancestry can also be a return to politics and understandings the state has worked hard to suppress. It can be a return to overlooked and underappreciated history.

There's a reason many of the communities already building forms of autonomy are facing the wrath of the state and the crisis of climate change. Resistance has placed them in the most vulnerable of positions. To attempt what I am suggesting here places us in the crosshairs of our adversaries and oppressors. We become a direct threat. It's no small thing, and it's not an easy undertaking. It will have to be sustained and defended.

CHAPTER FIVE

STATE OF WAR

*I'm not thinking about the government, any of them.... I'm here
for the people. My son will not die for nothing. Black people have
too much, too many resources, to let this white government
win every time.* —Samaria Rice (mother of Tamir Rice)

*A first-class citizen does not beg for freedom. A first-class citizen
does not plead to the white power-structure to give him something
that the whites have no power to give or take away. Human rights
are human rights, not white rights.* —Gloria Richardson

*I will never submit. The employment of the massive
coercive power of the state is not enough to make me give up;
I am like a Viet Cong—a Black Viet Cong.* —Martin Sostre

Fighting is unpleasant. Our survival requires cooperation, solidarity, and mutual aid but also involves overcoming obstacles. When
those obstacles are people, it means a fight. Winning may look like,
but not be limited to, true safety and peace for those of us who are
tired and worn. Fighting is the vehicle that carries us to a stability

that can seem unattainable at times. It takes all kinds of fighting, not just one type of effort. Unfortunately, though, some methods are overused in our movements, and they've become quite stale.

We must acknowledge the desperate search for a home within the current borders of the United States as a part of a larger conflict. Those in the most vulnerable positions understand this better than others. We're not pushed into conflict because we lack what some imagine to be good governance or leadership. We're pushed into this position precisely because of the "good" governance we are subject to in this country. Fighting is one of the results of trying to find comfort in the supposed security of an empire. Protection, peace, and healthy community are not guaranteed us in this country. To challenge all of these problems and more there has to be a significant confrontation that pushes beyond our present reality.

People often assign a certain cinematic quality to conflict, war, and revolution. Such idealized notions make it hard to think strategically in the here and now. White supremacists and the state are murdering us here and now. Prisons, detention centers, and police raids are confining and torturing us here and now. This, right here and right now, is what struggle looks like. Fantasizing about our fight happening in some heroic future leaves us disorganized and with little sense of agency in the present.

Living in the South, where I have spent most of my life, makes it hard to escape the fact that escalated conflict and perhaps another full-scale war are real possibilities. Ever since losing the Civil War, the former Confederacy has had a chip on its shoulder, which has led it to employ forms of domination that call into question whether it truly lost at all. It has sought to exercise as much violence as it could on Black people to prove a point regarding the nonevent of emancipation. As Saidiya Hartman writes, "emancipation instituted indebtedness," and its temporal attributes "bind one to the past, since what is owed draws the past into the present, and suspend the subject between what has been and what is." For Black America, "blame and duty and blood and dollars marked the birth of the free(d) subject."[1] The price we pay for an incomplete freedom is lives that can be taken or foreclosed on at any given moment. And even this is insufficient compensation for our enemies. Black people who didn't leave the South during the Great Migration have endured absolutely deplorable conditions. The terror of white supremacy has remained agitated and bitter in the South, hoping to remind Black people of their "place" in every way possible. That's not to say conditions for other Black people across the country haven't been bad. I only speak of a specific sort of experience in the South. It's one marked by flags, monuments, and legislation that are absolutely meant to convey an anti-Black message. That message

[1] Saidiya Hartman, *Scenes of Subjection: Terror, Slavery, and Self-Making in Nineteenth-Century America* (New York: Oxford University Press, 1997), 131.

has no border or boundary in the United States, but it's impossible to ignore its particular bold expressiveness in the South.

Those descendants of the Confederate army who embrace its legacy have never given up. They've only been lying in wait for their chance. There's no better place for people to understand this than the South. Generation after generation, children are trained in the aspirations of their Confederate forbears. "The South shall rise again" is not just a saying, it's a way of life and a battle cry for a cause that is supposedly not lost. They train, they shoot, and they are more than ready to kill at a moment's notice. This isn't a theory: it is the experience of the many Black people who have witnessed this reality up close. When you situate it next to a larger white suprema-cist movement that includes neo-fascist and white nationalist move-ments of all sorts, the present dangers become clearer. Furthermore, that's just *part* of the problem.

The state itself is white supremacist. The police and military are, in an important sense, merely the legitimate and institutionalized extension of social forces that, in other circumstances, would be called extremists. They are where the extremes of white supremacy, nationally and globally, become the norm. This extremism exists in some form at every level of government.

The election of Donald Trump, among other things, made as much clear for many who may have not yet realized what this coun-try is. And the racist millions who elected him have a comfortable stronghold in the South. The white dishonesty known as the Lost Cause is a part of the foundational work of the United Daughters of the Confederacy. The remnants of a disgruntled, defeated Confederacy became a form of perpetual propaganda. By dismissing the reality that the South had been fighting to maintain slavery and painting the Union as an aggressor, the white South has maintained a consistent narrative of victimhood. With the help of memorials, textbooks, and other concerted efforts to rewrite history, the sullen descendants of the Confederacy have been effective propagandists for years. Their twisted version of history is used to terrorize in the current day, because their past is not just the past; it's our horrific present. It's an instrument used to bludgeon the descendants of slavery's survivors as a reminder that the war is not quite over.

White supremacists in the South and beyond have committed themselves to revenge. The current psychological and physical terror that they inflict on Black people who live among them is just a taste of what they're capable of. By exonerating themselves from historical reality, they show themselves to be a vanguard for something much more insidious. This is not just about the rewrite; this is about the reigniting war. Until we recognize this, we remain perpetually vulnerable.

The United Daughters of the Confederacy was founded in 1894 and has been spreading their propaganda for well over a century now. This happens alongside the acts of physical violence and the continual preparation for further conflict that the white power structure engages in. Black people are not haunted by the specter of a possible race war: we are already living in one. Extrajudicial executions by police and state invasions in Black neighborhoods *are* the race war. They happen all across the country no matter where we live. Black people and other victims of white supremacy have experienced attacks ranging from biological warfare to all-out military assaults. White supremacists and fascists of all sorts long for their chance to escalate into all-out war so they can go about a wholesale slaughter. The question remains, what would those of us who are targeted do?

If there was open warfare raging in the streets tomorrow, how would we defend ourselves? Would we take the liberal approach and try to talk our enemies out of killing us? Would we even know how to fight, shoot, stab, or flee if necessary? Do we know how to survive in nature if we have to hide? The questions are endless. However, it's worth asking them because the people who want to kill us have been thinking about this and *practicing this* for a very long time. Recent years have brought things to our attention that many of us have never imagined, and fascists and their militias speak openly about this while they patrol the streets. Surely there are some radicals who actively think about these things, but the left is severely underprepared in this regard. Conversations about conflict and self-defense are often abstract and hollow, if they happen at all. This is a recipe for a massacre.

On some level, Black people throughout the Western world have understood that we are experiencing versions of statelessness in the midst of ongoing state violence and conflict for some time. For many, it has often meant placing oneself in the position of a foreigner or outsider. Black people have consistently chosen to take up arms against Western states others might see as their own to defend. The truth is simple: if you're Black, none of it is yours, no matter how high a position you hold serving the state or in an oppressive class. Participating or aiding the onslaught against your own people doesn't even guarantee your safety, no more so than saying the Pledge of Allegiance or joining the imperialist armed forces do. Reflecting on post-9/11 politics, Angela Davis has said that "nationalism always requires an enemy—whether inside or outside the nation." As she sees it, "the production of the nation as the primary mode of solidarity excluded those within and without who were not legally citizens."[2] Seeing how Blackness complicates and impairs even formal citizenship, the same enemy status is implicitly applied to Black people who are incapable of securing the protections of citizenship. We are Black outsiders, and we are seen as enemy combatants or enemies of the state by a security apparatus that views us a perpetual threat.

The Black incompatibility with citizenship here is often obvious when viewed from outside the U.S. empire. For that reason, foreign

[2] Angela Y. Davis, *Abolition Democracy: Beyond Empire, Prisons, and Torture* (New York: Seven Stories Press, 2005), 42.

powers have sometimes made appeals to occupying Black soldiers and Black people back home to "betray" the U.S. government. However, given the extra-state location our Blackness imposes on us, what would we actually be betraying if we fought back against the U.S. state? How can a Black person commit treason if they're not considered true citizens? Of course, the state will always view us as treasonous based on our identity alone, but our own understanding that we'll never really reap the benefits of citizenship should help us redefine our concept of "betrayal" and reprioritize our commitments. For many Black people, sedition is survival and survival is seditious.

We are consequently prime suspects, and our day-to-day movements will always look like sedition to the pervasive anti-Black state "security" structure monitoring our everyday lives. Those who dare challenge the legitimacy of the state will always be accused of colluding with foreign governments or betraying the country. The perpetual attack on us takes many forms, from surveillance to ever more invasive policing to literal military assaults on whatever safe havens we've managed to create. Being Black positions us as a treasonous antistate threat creating a continual cycle of disruption and antagonism that Black people, whatever our politics, can never fully escape.

Black people do not have to be radicals to be heavily monitored. Our politics are not the sole indicator of the state's pressing need to observe our movements. Simone Browne traces surveillance back to the slave trade and and notes the state's racialized practice of it. She discusses how biometric systems privilege and empower whiteness and lightness today and connects this back as far as colonial New York City "lantern laws," which "sought to keep the black, the mixed-race, and indigenous body in a state of permanent illumination."[3] As she describes it, Black people were once required to carry lanterns then to keep themselves visible at night and could be punished if they failed to obey. Browne thus establishes a direct line from modern practices like stop-and-frisk to forms of anti-Black state supervision practiced since the earliest days of this country.

That constant need to monitor and police the Black population underscores the intentions of the irreformable state and our location as noncitizen "foreigners" no matter where we reside here. It shows us that this place is not a home at all for us, it is a series of problems. The authorities know we're being antagonized. It's not an accident. We have to be visible so that the state can attack us as needed. We must be recognizable and identifiable for the sake of enslavement or imprisonment, extrajudicial killing, and infiltration. As perpetual enemies of the state, anything we do can be seen as a threat. Even Black people working as state operatives can't escape their Black-

[3] Simone Browne, *Dark Matters: On the Surveillance of Blackness* (Durham, NC: Duke University Press, 2015), 67.

ness through the benefit of authority. Diversity and inclusion in state power do not and will not stop our neighborhoods from being sites of state violence and assault.

Warrantless wiretapping, relatively easy access to tech giants' servers, and collection of our communication data present special challenges for those of us whose very existence is suspect and revokable by the state. Over time, Black people have been given no choice but to circumvent and reject borders, prisons, and police, both physical and digital.

The police have become increasingly reliant on lethal robotics. Drone warfare dominates headlines while police departments test out semi-autonomous and autonomous robots that can patrol, pursue, and worse. We must remember that Black people are a prime domestic testing site for new technologies of war. The Black neighborhood is where the police state thrives, though it's not strictly contained here.

History gives us plenty of examples of Black neighborhoods being transformed into conflict zones whenever we step outside the roles assigned to us, try to establish our autonomy, or even just live. The 1921 destruction of the bustling, successful Black community of Greenwood (also known to many for its "Black Wall Street") in Tulsa, Oklahoma, by police who were working with white civilian mobs, involved aerial bombing and machine-gun fire. Both were then fairly new forms of war technology. Bombing would go on to be a regular occurrence for Black people. It defined Birmingham, Alabama, prior to and during the civil rights movement to the extent that it was dubbed "Bombingham" and included a neighborhood known as "Dynamite Hill," where Black people were forced to defend against frequent attacks with explosives.

All too often, cities with large Black populations experience state-sanctioned assaults. The 1967 uprising in Detroit was one of many such confrontations, this one between residents of Black neighborhoods and the Detroit Police Department, with the governor adding the Michigan National Guard and President Lyndon Johnson sending in the U.S. Army's 82nd and 101st Airborne Divisions. The city was transformed by occupying forces. Under the designation "race riots," Black people have long defended against the ongoing invasions we've experienced at the hands of state forces. The same dynamic could be seen in the rebellions that took place following the 1968 assassination of Dr. Martin Luther King Jr. in cities around the country. When it comes to Black resistance and anarchistic tendencies, we also cannot neglect the 1985 MOVE bombing in Philadelphia.

MOVE was founded in Philadelphia under the direction of John Africa in 1972 as a Black liberation organization. The group set itself apart by operating according to its own ideas of environmentalism, self-defense, health, and even personal relationships. Their beliefs, which combined spirituality, ecology, and opposition to systemic in-

The childhood home of Angela Davis
on "Dynamite Hill" in Birmingham

justice, directly challenged many notions of what was and wasn't appropriate according to mainstream society. Its members still promote what they call "Natural Law" as opposed to "Man-made laws [that] ... require police, sheriffs, armies, and courts to enforce them, and lawyers to explain them."[4]

This became a point of contention with the city as members enacted their principles in their West Philadelphia neighborhood. MOVE suffered from a variety of attacks and enclosures aimed at forcing them to leave their place of residence and disperse. They were met with police violence time and time again. In 1978, this escalated into an armed confrontation that saw the imprisonment of nine members (the MOVE 9). Speaking of the these, imprisoned activist and journalist Mumia Abu-Jamal said, "They were convicted of being united, not in crime, but in rebellion against the system and in resistance to the armed assaults of the State."[5] The standoff between MOVE and the state reached a climax in 1985 under the leadership of the first Black mayor of Philadelphia, W. Wilson Goode Sr., who classified MOVE a terrorist organization and allowed police to drop a bomb on their home, killing eleven members (including five children) and destroying over sixty homes on two city blocks.

[4] MOVE Organization, "About Move," On a MOVE, onamove.com/about.

[5] Mumia Abu Jamal, "The Move 9; 26 Yrs. in Hell," *Prison Radio*, August 8, 2004, archive.prisonradio.org/maj/maj_8_8_04move.html.

More recently, uprisings against police brutality have taken place across the United States in cities like Baltimore, Minneapolis, and Ferguson, Missouri. For Black people, the war is and has always been here at "home," and efficient weaponry will be used against us as enemies of the state, regardless of any cosmetic, liberal efforts to create an appearance of addressing our extrajudicial assassination by police. Various Black anarchistic and Black autonomous politics can help us assess and respond to our situation and begin thinking of ways to defend ourselves in the war that is already happening all around us and in the wars that are to come. Our oppressors don't want to think of new ways to coexist; they only want new ways to kill. We don't have to suffer silently or await the next casualty.

To fully understand the logic and purpose of the police—and of the state that enables them—we must consider both their origins and the future that their actions point toward. The police we know today arose as slave catchers and night watchmen, taking on additional violent roles over history. In 1757, Georgia's colonial assembly passed "An Act for Establishing and Regulating of Patrols" in an effort to prevent any Black insurrections. Modeled on similar legislation in South Carolina, it involved a sort of proto-stop-and-frisk. White men on patrol were empowered to demand identification and explanations from any Black people they encountered, much like the police today. White landowners and residents were required to serve on patrols, though the wealthy landowners could afford to hire substitutes for themselves. After a while, it became necessary to pay all patrol members. According to the *New Georgia Encyclopedia*, "Slave patrols had the legal right to enter, without warrant, the plantation grounds of any Georgian; they often searched the slave quarters and inspected slave homes, looking for stolen goods, missing slaves who had turned runaway, weapons that could be used in an insurrection, or evidence of literacy and education, including books, papers, and pens (teaching a slave to read was forbidden by Georgia law in the antebellum period)." Over time, the duties of these patrollers "merged with those associated with modern-day policemen and firemen: patrollers investigated strange circumstances (moving lights in a warehouse at night, rowdy gatherings in drinking dens, anyone who acted suspiciously)."[6]

This portion of the state's forces has long engaged us in ongoing attacks. Black people have often chosen to meet oppressive violence with forms of self-defense. If we haven't already, it is time to ask ourselves what we're doing and what's at stake. Given the nature of the increasing gap between those who have and those who do not and the disasters of the climate crisis, we know the planet is in complete turmoil. What does completely separating ourselves from it all look like?

[6] Sally E. Hadden, "Slave Patrols," *New Georgia Encyclopedia*, May 14, 2003, https://www.georgiaencyclopedia.org/articles/history-archaeology/slave-patrols.

Saying "stop killing us" and asking an oppressor not to oppress is not going to work. Taking the life of the system we're up against through abolition is much more complex than simply fighting people in the streets. We need to eradicate the very structures that enable the state to continue systematically destroying our lives. Oppression tortures our existence through the forces that live comfortably in the minds of countless people they oppress. The conflicts created and exacerbated by the oppressive mechanics of the state are not evenly distributed. Some neighborhoods and some people within our communities know destruction in intimate ways that involve infighting and traumatic violence. Black women and girls—especially those who are queer, transgender, poor, and disabled—experience this in the most extreme forms, with their very right to survive called into question. "What the law designated as crime," writes Saidiya Hartman "were the forms of life created by young black women in the city."[7] If these women and girls defend themselves, they are criminalized for it, as abolitionist Mariame Kaba documented in the anthology *No Selves to Defend*.[8] Therefore, women and girls in this

[7] Saidiya Hartman, *Wayward Lives, Beautiful Experiments: Intimate Histories of Riotous Black Girls, Troublesome Women, and Queer Radicals* (New York: W. W. Norton, 2019), 236.

[8] Mariame Kaba, *No Selves to Defend: A Legacy of Criminalizing Women of Color for Self Defense* (self-published, 2014), noselves2defend.wordpress.com.

predicament have been a primary basis for my conception of self-defense, community, and survival amid conflict.

In *As Black as Resistance*, Zoé Samudzi and I touched on "Black gangs that were born of necessity and are often far better organized than those who denounce them would ever give them credit for."[9] We also noted that these gangs had been politicized at the same time as the social struggles in the 1960s and 1970s and became part of the movement for self-defense and community control. It bears repeating that we shouldn't ignore gangs and others who have been shunned as we think through these questions.

What does it mean, for instance, to strengthen our communities and build survival programs, when there is no functioning left opposition in the United States that could defend them against militarized police forces, fascist militias, and military assaults? Just because reactionary forces have not freely carried out the full-scale massacres of large numbers of unarmed people all at once, it doesn't mean they never will. If (or when) that time should come—and if Black people manage to wrest real political and economic autonomy for ourselves, it will—many people will need to know how to fight back.

People imagine history's revolutions, rebellions, and insurrections in such an idealistic way that they become fairy tales that re-

---

[9] Zoé Samudzi and William C. Anderson, *As Black as Resistance: Finding the Conditions for Liberation* (Chico, CA: AK Press, 2018), 53.

quire magic wishes more than training or planning. As our enemies stockpile, plot, and prepare, far too many act as if merely our love of liberatory ideas will save us. As it often has been throughout Black history, armed self-defense should become more of a serious consideration in the future. We will not be given a choice. Those who are most familiar with fighting in the streets are needed too, which will require people to look beyond the trauma and the stigma of "criminality." Such transformations should recognize and center the experiences of the women, children, sex workers, and other community members who have borne the brunt of violence. This means we must also address how regularly they must protect themselves from the likes of gangs and the militaristic, patriarchal violence that creates constant clashes. Like the gangs, they know how to fight and resist and defend themselves in ways many of us can learn from.

There are many potential allies out there with the knowledge that pontificating radicals on the left lack. Those people might or might not identify as part of the organized left. We shouldn't feed into the vanguardist binary that makes "the people" who don't identify as leftists or radicals into masses in need of leadership. Our respective stories and different struggles will vary from community to community. No one should be carelessly left behind. We also have much to learn from revolutionaries who preceded us and were discarded at times themselves.

Assata Shakur, Lorenzo Kom'boa Ervin, Malcolm X, and George Jackson are just a few examples of hugely impactful people who were designated "criminal." Their militancy or willingness to address questions of actual confrontation cannot be separated from how they understood the realities of the streets. By the same token, there are many young Black people in the streets, alienated from social movements but with needed energy for liberatory politics. There is certainly crucial organizing to be done among members of groups that get left out of the conversations of both the left and the mainstream nonprofit organizations in the process of movement building.

When we look to our families, many of us will find a history of organized self-defense there too. For one thing, many of the Black anarchists and radicals I've mentioned are former members of the military, including Martin Sostre, Lorenzo Kom'boa Ervin, Kuwasi Balagoon, and others in the Black Panther Party. Each of them enlisted with different histories and brought back their own lessons. Balagoon, for instance, was a bisexual man in the U.S. Army. His experience—who he was and who he became—informed the militancy he later engaged in with the Black Liberation Army. There are others like him among us who also carry knowledge and understanding of warfare that we should familiarize ourselves with. Understanding this doesn't mean embracing imperialism or the military. I am referring simply to information and strategic thinking that should be taken into consideration based on our circumstances.

We are not talking about fighting for the sake of fighting; it's about the larger political goal of achieving liberation. Recent uprisings and rebellions we've seen have often lacked organized self-defense components. At the same time, many of the armed self-defense mobilizations we see today are showy demonstrations of symbolic force unconnected to actual communities in struggle—parades and marches that defend nothing. The task of revolutionaries, as Lorenzo Ervin has explained, is to "push rebellions to [an] insurrectionary stage, and the insurrection to a social revolution."[10] War is not coming. War is already here all around us, and we're already engaged, systematically, as casualties. To change that takes planning and preparation and direct confrontation.

If we're waiting for the worst to happen every time, we should expect defeat. In fact, we're beating ourselves. Our advancement requires a proactive effort to abolish the violent institutions of the white supremacist state. Black anarchism reveals to us that revolution and war are about killing concepts that do us damage, the forces that many of us face every day when we go outside. We're at war with white supremacy, sexism, homophobia, transphobia, ableism, and more.

So, if we understand history and the possibility of warfare in

---

[10] Lorenzo Kom'boa Ervin, *Anarchism and the Black Revolution*, theanar chistlibrary.org/library/lorenzo-kom-boa-ervin-anarchism-and-the-black-revolution.

front of us, we're required to respond. This means, yes, as many of us as are willing need to be prepared to learn about weapons and be prepared to use them to defend ourselves if or when it becomes necessary. But we have to understand security at every level and learn how to avoid and protect ourselves from every attack. Liberation begins in our communities: if we cannot protect them at the ground level, our work and our efforts will collapse. Masses of people do not need to be squeezed into one specific soldiering role: some people caretake, some cook, some organize, some clean, some make art, some teach, and so on. However, we do need many who are training and preparing consistently with whatever tools they have. The alternative is our demise. Unless we've given up, we have work to do.

Running from state to state, nation to nation, and empire to empire hoping for more is not a way to live. Many people speak of decolonization, but we should heed the words of Frantz Fanon who made it very clear that "decolonization is always a violent event."[11] As he put it: "Decolonization, which sets out to change the order of the world, is, obviously, a program of complete disorder. But it cannot come as a result of magical practices, nor of a natural shock, nor of a friendly understanding. Decolonization, as we know, is a historical process: that is to say that it cannot be understood, it can-

[11] Frantz Fanon, *The Wretched of the Earth* (New York: Grove Press, 2004), I.

not become intelligible nor clear to itself except in the exact measure that we can discern the movements that give it historical form and content."[12]

This term has grown increasingly popular and is often irresponsibly thrown around in a manner that loses sight both of the inherent *conflict* involved and the need to understand decolonization as a historical process rather than some simple declaration. There are very real, often very physical confrontations that come with revolt, with establishing one's place in history, especially when the world as you know it has decided that you don't belong *anywhere*. How can we map out where we're supposed to be if we cannot locate ourselves in the mire of violence? The politics of Black anarchism can mean fighting from where we are, no matter where that is.

Stay and fight, or leave—this is the internal debate that Black people have historically been forced to have. Moving—to a new neighborhood, a new country, or a new social class—or staying put to struggle for more, these mirror the options faced by Black people over generations when the idea of "escaping to freedom" seemed possible. We can now see: the only place to run is nowhere.

Understanding this "nowhere" means comprehending statelessness. If the state offers us no home as Black people, why not reject it as a concept wholeheartedly? The same goes for capitalism, polic-

[12] Ibid, 2.

ing, prisons, and so on. If we are forced to ask "Who will survive in America?" then perhaps "America" does not need to survive.[13] Far from a burden, there is something immediately liberating about admitting to ourselves that we are not a part of this country and that we shouldn't commit ourselves to protecting a fantasy that has had centuries to prove it's anything more than that. We must fight against the state, not ourselves. We are not the state, just as people around the world are not the state apparatuses that draw borders around them—though some derive greater benefits from them than others.

Those who are stuck in an inability to honestly engage with and discern the past will continually fail in the present. In order to begin writing new liberatory histories, we must address and bring an end to the old, oppressive ones.[14] This psychological break is just as much a part of the fight as any other confrontation associated with abolishing the white supremacist state. Black people don't need some vanguard to guide them to this understanding. We know it at some level already, but the temptation and desires to try to clutch at easy, stale concepts is always there.

[13] In Gil Scott Heron's spoken-word poem "Comment #1" on the 1970 album *Small Talk at 125th and Lenox*, he repeatedly asks "Who will survive in America?"

[14] Fanon writes, "The immobility to which the colonized subject is condemned can be challenged only if he decides to put an end to the history of colonization and the history of despoliation in order to bring to life the history of the nation, the history of decolonization." Fanon, *The Wretched of the Earth*, 15.

The idea that we must play along with existing nation-states or become one ourselves will present itself time and time again. The struggle to achieve liberation and create something new can be scary. Some people will inevitably suggest models that are just repackaged versions of what we're trying to escape. And even many of those are far more of a fantasy than anything I've proposed.

Any state that Black people would attempt to build would be considered a "rogue state" on the current world stage, something to be eliminated by empire and other competing states. This happens even at a local level, as we've seen with MOVE and as we saw decades ago with countless Black Panther Party chapters around the country. As we saw in Tulsa, even attempts to *collectively* establish economic autonomy within a capitalist framework have to be attacked and destroyed. *Individual* attempts might be rewarded with fame and wealth, but white supremacy necessitates the destruction of Black communities that make even the slightest move toward becoming autonomous, semi-autonomous, or even self-sufficient under the terms and conditions of the racist U.S. state. This shouldn't stop us from attempting to establish ourselves, but it should challenge us to think beyond the terms of the world that's been established at our expense.

Thinking through the challenges at hand, we must encourage movements much more radical than what we're currently seeing. The lack of an organized radical opposition has made it so bad that each state escalation isn't met with enough outrage. There is a need for even more. When outrage and some form of action beyond symbolic protests *do* happen, as they have after many high-profile police killings, they're often fleeting, disjointed, and settle quickly into inactivity until the next atrocity. But still, far too many people respond with passivity and acceptance of the violence that surrounds us. Masses of people feel helpless, wonder what they can do—and come up with nothing. Organizers, activists, and those who care can no longer afford to let this happen. Ecocidal destruction certainly makes it imperative that we promote radical solutions to our problems, while organizing and preparing for the worst. Many people aren't going to fully realize how bad things can get until the fight is at their door (if it isn't already), and by then it could be too late for some. And as Camille Yarborough has forewarned, "when they come to get us people, don't talk about no Bill of Rights."[15]

The work of developing politicized people who can organize and manage themselves is of the utmost importance in building a sustainable future for ourselves. This is another reason we shouldn't concern ourselves with state-making. The nation-state is *always* going to be a destructive project by any reasonable measure of justice or equality, not to mention in terms of undoing white supremacy. A

[15] Camille Yarbrough, *The Iron Pot Cooker* (Vanguard, 1975). Rereleased on CD in 1999.

Bethel Street Baptist Church was bombed

"successful" state in this world requires domination, and that is precisely the logic we're trying to escape. Powerful states rely on the existence of weak and "developing" states that they can exploit and maintain hegemony and control over. Trying to create a Black state makes about as much sense as promoting Black billionaires or corporations to fight the onslaught of capitalism, but some people remain determined to draw inspiration from nonsense.

Black people having conservative and reactionary responses to white supremacy is not entirely surprising. The brutality of the fight we're engaged in encourages such reactions, and, since white supremacy is ubiquitous and seemingly unending, some people will simply want a share of the power it offers, a seat at the table of injustice. This is where much of the desire to create a Black nation-state arises from and why it often goes uncontested. This can make for some disturbing alliances, and it is critical that we should be aware of historical parallels.

In a 1937 interview, Marcus Garvey spoke about the Universal Negro Improvement Association (UNIA) saying, "We were the first Fascists. We had disciplined men, women and children in training for the liberation of Africa. The black masses saw that in this extreme nationalism lay their only hope and readily supported it. Mussolini copied fascism from me but the Negro reactionaries sabotaged it."[16]

[16] Quoted in Paul Gilroy, "Black Fascism," *Transition*, no. 81/82 (2000): 70.

Garvey's belief that he inspired fascism cannot be painted over in favor of an ideal historical portrait. Garvey also met and negotiated with white supremacist forces like the Ku Klux Klan. "They are," he said, "honest and honorable in their desire to purify and preserve the white race even as we are determined to purify and standardize our race."[17] As Paul Gilroy writes, "Garvey's views are part of a nationalist vision supported by the familiar masculine values of conquest and military prowess."[18] He quotes Garvey explaining his understanding of genocidal white supremacist state: "This is a white man's country. He found it, he conquered it and we can't blame him because he wants to keep it. I'm not vexed with the white man of the South for Jim Crowing me because I am black. I never built any street cars or railroads. The white man built them for their own convenience. And if I don't want to ride where he's willing to let me then I'd better walk."[19]

We could write these statements off as peculiar and irrational takes if some version of their logic wasn't embraced today. There are contemporary Black nationalists who still idolize this aspect of Garvey much like the authoritarian left worships at the feet of their sainted authoritarian leaders. These views manifest themselves to-

[17] Ibid., 71.
[18] Ibid.
[19] Ibid.

day not simply in the uncritical acceptance of the idea of nationhood but also in other rigid conservatism that lectures to us about identity, family structure, and morality. This sort of ideology makes oppression invisible and subtly blames its victims for personal shortcomings and a lack of discipline. This understanding finds new life in some of the groups we see around us today.

The American Descendants of Slavery (ADOS) hope to "reclaim/restore the critical national character of the African American identity and experience, one grounded in our group's unique lineage, and which is central to our continuing struggle for social and economic justice in the United States."[20] In an attempt to receive reparations for slavery from the government, ADOS has created a nativist and nationalist program of Black separation based on "lineage" rather than shared oppression under the white supremacist state. According to their "Black Agenda," existing affirmative action should be "streamlined as a government program only and specifically for ADOS," that is, for "eligible recipients from gathered data."[21] Black people in the United States would be divided into those who can "provide reasonable documentation of at least

[20] "About ADOS," American Descendants of Slavery, ados101.com/about-ados.

[21] "Black Agenda," American Descendants of Slavery, ados101.com/black-agenda.

one ancestor enslaved" and those who can't.[22] Black people have been migrating and forced to relocate inside and outside of U.S. borders ever since slavery, but ADOS's logic freezes Black Americans in a customized myth of origin. Enslaved people were not always brought directly to a final destination and left there; they were regularly traded as human property and shipped from country to country. ADOS ignores this to embrace the U.S. flag that has terrorized Black people in favor of a narrow "American" identity based on artificial boundaries. As a result, their efforts end up shoring up the state that has been working nonstop for our destruction. The U.S. state would have to pay with its very existence for the immeasurable harms committed against Black people over the centuries, and that *still* wouldn't be enough.

ADOS isn't the only troubling group. Other groups mix militancy with their efforts to spread their toxic nationalism. Following the death of Black Panther Party leader Huey P. Newton, the New Black Panther Party (NBPP) emerged. It has become a favorite for conservative pundits and media trying to portray a fear-mongering version of Black radicals as destructive agents driven by an unrelenting hatred of white people. Its membership has offered plenty of material to support that case, affirming themselves as disturbingly big-

[22] "The Roadmap to Reparations," American Descendants of Slavery, ados101.com/roadmap-to-reparations.

oted, antisemitic, and right-wing. Founding member of the original Black Panther Party, Elbert "Big Man" Howard denounced the group as "strutting caricatures" and "a collective of racist, reactionary thugs and tools of the still-very-much-alive Cointelpro government agency."[23] Lorenzo Kom'boa Ervin has addressed the formation of groups like the New Black Panther Party on the grounds of their romanticized posturing militancy that accomplishes far less than the original Black Panther Party. He encourages such groups to reject sexism, militarism, racism, and cultism or else disband, because they are in effect "zealots" and "political opportunists" hijacking a legacy.

Then there's also the case of the Nation of Islam (NOI). Founded in 1930, the NOI set a standard for Black nationalism that would attract the hearts and minds of many Black celebrities, activists, politicians, and more.[24] The NOI is based on messianic lead-

[23] Elbert Howard, "Concerning Reactionaries and Thugs: The New Black Panther Party," *San Francisco Bay View*, August 23, 2015.

[24] In *Black Fascism*, Paul Gilroy points out that rapper Ice Cube has been heavily involved with the Nation of Islam. Ice Cube also attempted to negotiate a "Contract with Black America" plan. He revealed that he'd been in conversation with ADOS leading up to the 2020 election when he hoped to negotiate with the Trump administration to secure a large sum of money that would essentially have been a payoff. In one section of the infantilizing contract titled "Black Responsibility," it states, "This contract is a 2-way street. As we gain social and economic equality, we must begin to dissolve any bitterness in our hearts for past

ership and a clear nationalist impulse that has created offspring of other organizations and movements like it. Ashanti Alston, in his essay "Beyond Nationalism but Not Without It," describes the Nation of Islam's leader Louis Farrakhan somewhat favorably:

> For me, even the nationalism of a Louis Farrakhan is about saving my people, though it is also thoroughly sexist, capitalist, homophobic and potentially fascist. Yet, it has played an important part in keeping a certain black pride and resistance going. Their "on the ground" work is very important in keeping an anti-racist mentality going. As a black anarchist, that's MY issue to deal with cuz they'se MY FOLKS. But it points to where anarchism and nationalism have differences: most anarchists in the U.S. have NO understanding of what it means to be BLACK in this fucked up society. We do not have the luxury of being so intellectual about this excruciating boot on our collective neck, this modern-day middle-passage into the Prison Industrial Complex and other forms of neo-slavery.[25]

---

wrongs. We must become better citizens who are more productive on all levels of American society." See "Ice Cube Demands Politicians Sign Contract with Black America Before Getting Support of Black Vote," Cision PR Newswire, www.prnewswire.com/news-releases/ice-cube-demands-politicians-sign-contract-with-black-america-before-getting-support-of-black-vote-301116710.html.

[25] Ashanti Alston, "Beyond Nationalism but Not Without It," *Onward* 2, no. 4 (Spring 2002): 10–11.

Alston may be right that they are "our issue" to deal with, which, for me, means opposing "potentially fascist" arrangements. Black nationalism like that of the NOI furthers the sexism, homophobia, and transphobia that contribute to deadly conditions that require many Black people to defend themselves from the state *and* in their own homes and neighborhoods. Yes, I believe that we must move beyond Black nationalism, but I also believe that we can certainly move forward without it too. Martin Sostre's evolution in this regard is illuminating. He was in the Nation of Islam while in prison but parted ways when he observed a new radicalism among Black youth after he was released. He embraced his role as radical educator, opening the radical Afro-Asian Book Shop in Buffalo, New York. When the state locked him up again (on charges later proven to be fabricated), he crossed paths with Lorenzo Kom'boa Ervin and introduced him to anarchism. His breaking away represents a radical growth that helps us observe the limitations of nationalism and that led to the earliest foundations of contemporary Black anarchism.

Still, the nationalism question can complicate and show the limits of even some versions of Black anarchism. Some are open to forms of Black nationalism that some white anarchists reject out of hand, either because they see no difference between nationalism and statism or, in some cases, out of a racist fear of Black autonomy. Certainly, we cannot conflate the fascism of white supremacy and empire with that which responds to it, even if that response mimics some of the destructive reasoning of its oppressor. The two must be addressed as distinct issues. Alston's embrace of Black nationalism stems from his origins in the Black Panther Party, which often based politicization on certain forms of Black pride. However, there are also risks that come with this, risks that can cost us everything if we do not engage in reflective critique. The Black anarchists and radicals who left the Black Panther Party and the NOI did so because of issues around aspects of the nationalist rationale. At various points, Black anarchists like Lorenzo Kom'boa Ervin, Ashanti Alston, and Kuwasi Balagoon, among others, have had differing relationships to the idea of Black nationalism in its various forms.

But the NOI has very disturbing history here that requires our full attention. Before Malcolm X was murdered, the NOI sent him on a mission to discuss with the Ku Klux Klan the idea of securing land to which Black people might migrate.[26] The NOI also went as far as to allow the leadership of the American Nazi Party to attend their 1962 convention. These incidents are not completely separate from the legacy of Marcus Garvey's and UNIA's back-to-Africa movement.

Even before Garvey, though, there were efforts to turn Black

[26] See Les Payne and Amanda Payne, *The Dead Are Arising: The Life of Malcolm X* (New York: W. W. Norton, 2020). This story is told in Chapter 13.

people in the United States into an uprooted nation, with all the disastrous effects that one might expect from such an effort when it's not actually a new, revolutionary social formation. Beginning in 1816, the American Colonization Society sought to create a colony on the African continent to send away increasing numbers of formerly enslaved Black people in the United States. This effort wasn't Black-led, and it involved collaboration with white supremacists who were happy to send thousands of Black people to the colony that ultimately, in 1847, became Liberia. The Black Americans (Americo-Liberians) eventually developed political power and established hierarchies that excluded, exploited, and disenfranchised native people. Black settlers from the United States asserted control through authority and governance that legitimized their rule, creating models of dominance that were inspired by the U.S. South. Sylvester A. Johnson describes it this way:

> Within a decade of Liberia's beginnings, the Black Christian settlers solidified their racial governance over native Africans, thereby crafting a regime of freedom to benefit themselves. This included forcing recaptured native Africans to work through indenture to Americo-Liberians. By 1847 the polity celebrated its official independence as a sovereign republic, a Black Christian settler state functioning as a constitutional democracy rooted in popular sovereignty. What emerged, in other words, was a system of minority rule born of violent conquest. That con-

quest grounded a political economy operating under the sign of freedom to achieve self-determination for a population who had been stateless in the US republic.[27]

If the UNIA had been successful, Garvey's conservative vision could have had a similar fate. Examples like this show the dangerous potential of states, even in the hands of people who look like us. Cedric Robinson explains the distinctly nonrevolutionary characteristics of Garvey's goals:

> The UNIA's main thrust appears to have been toward the development of a powerful Black nation economically organized by a modified form of capitalism. This powerful entity was to become the guardian of the interests of Blacks in Africa (where it was to be located) and those dispersed in the African diaspora. The nation was to be founded on a technocratic elite recruited from the Black peoples of the world. This elite, in turn, would create the structures necessary for the nation's survival and its development until it was strong enough to play its historical role and absorb and generate subsequent generations of trained, disciplined nationalists.[28]

[27] Sylvester A. Johnson, *African American Religions, 1500–2000: Colonialism, Democracy, and Freedom* (Cambridge: Cambridge University Press, 2015), 206.

[28] Cedric J. Robinson, *Black Marxism: The Making of the Black Radical Tradition* (Chapel Hill: University of North Carolina Press, 2000), 214.

We can see what the past has become in the present. Fantastical narratives of Black people as quasi-supernatural disinherited royalty whose Blackness alone makes them worthy and capable have thus far failed to help us secure liberation. We must read our history. When it relies on nation-building, capitalism, and a sense of inherent righteousness, it has led to dead ends or worse. Gilroy notes that in these dangerous forms of nationalism there is a strange notion of innocence:

> The myths of essential innocence shield their supposed beneficiaries from the complex moral choices that define human experience and insulate them from the responsibility to act well and choose wisely. This kind of thinking would usher black politics into a desert: a flattened moral landscape bereft of difficult decisions, where cynicism would rule effortlessly in the guise of naturalized morality. Hidden within that exaltation of biologically grounded innocence is a promise that the political lives of the innocent will eventually be emancipated from moral constraint. Innocence makes the difficult work of judgment and negotiation irrelevant. And wherever that innocence is inflated by the romance of "race," nationhood, and ethnic fraternity, fascism will flourish.
>
> The capacity to perpetrate evil is not a modern phenomenon, but the scale and power of the modern nation-state expand and condition it.[29]

[29] Gilroy, "Black Fascism," 91.

Nationalism and embrace of autocratic, fascistic, and authoritarian tendencies will not help us overcome the barriers imposed by the white supremacist state. Nationhood is not a solution because the nation-state carries the ability to cause immeasurable harm. Like a despot or political leader who justifies their long reign and cements their place in office repeatedly, the nation-state always justifies its existence and authority to do the same. Whatever Black nationalists have been able to accomplish was done by masses of people, not individuals. Those masses are erased in the biographies of allegedly great men. The nation stands above the people, when it is the people themselves who must take responsibility. Discussing "the trials and tribulations of national consciousness," Fanon provides further clarity on this point. "To politicize the masses is not and cannot be to make a political speech. It means driving home to the masses that everything depends on them, that if we stagnate the fault is theirs, and that if we progress, they too are responsible, that there is no demiurge, no illustrious man taking responsibility for everything, but that the demiurge is the people and the magic lies in their hands and their hands alone."[30]

This is a process of locating ourselves both literally and figuratively. Where we are on the map relates directly to our intentions, goals, and how we build radical, liberatory movements that actually

[30] Fanon, *The Wretched of the Earth*, 138.

shape our future for the better. Whatever our future looks like, we cannot endanger other people's safety, security, or the planet while we try to sort out our situation. The answer to state violence is not a new or reformed state, it's operating beyond and surpassing the expired relevance of such a destructive formation. In the process of us locating ourselves and finding our position as Black people in precarious conditions, we cannot discount the effectiveness of the deceptions around us that try to draw us back into limited patterns of thought.

We're talking about creating an entirely new world. However, even though we're unwilling to accept this one, we are sometimes intolerant about the idea of creating a new one. We somehow think that more of the same, with slight adjustments or reforms, will get us somewhere different. Even people who would stand to benefit can hate the idea of a complete rupture. Change can cause fear, including the fear of losing what little you already have. But we have to press on because, as things currently stand, we're dying. The process may be more delayed or expedited depending on where we stand in terms of class, identity, or geography, but we're *still* dying. We can't let it continue any longer. If we are willing to admit that there is nowhere to escape state violence on this empire-covered planet and that we're in a perpetual state of war simply because of who we are, then certain ways forward become clear.

The ruined New Manchester Manufacturing Company

CHAPTER SIX

RUINATION

The hope is that return could resolve the old dilemmas,
make a victory out of defeat, and engender a new order.
And the disappointment is that there is no going back to
a former condition. Loss remakes you. —Saidiya Hartman

If destroying all the maps known / would erase all the boundaries /
from the face of this earth / I would say let us / make a bonfire /
to reclaim and sing / the human person —Keorapetse Kgositsile

We were not brought here to be made citizens. —Malcolm X

Black anarchism calls for us to abandon state-building, including our hopes to reform existing states. This means asking people to reconsider the idea that incremental changes will inevitably lead us to a revolutionary freedom. We have to ask: when is enough enough? The politics of Black anarchism are not interested in trying to repair or reform the state; they call for its abolition. The question of liberation can be deferred and delayed right up to the point that an enormous confrontation stares us directly in the face, but why wait until that point? Why wait for the sound of an officer's gun, the sound of a closing cell, or the pinch of a lethal injection? Delaying the question can generate the sort of nervousness a prisoner feels waiting to hear if a stay of execution has been temporarily granted. It leads to a bewilderment about why we have let them get away with so much, as we're evicted, killed, driven into debt, and stolen from. It means feeling hopeless as election cycles repeat themselves to the point that the gap between promises and realities makes us ill with disappointment. We can wait while this wretched machinery continues to do its work or we can destroy the gears.

This is a process of destruction. It is about bringing forth a *complete* ruination—not ours, but the total dismantling of the white supremacist state and all the institutions that keep us subjugated. This is the *opposite* of seeking inclusion and reform. We must create beautiful ventures that can no longer be co-opted and taken away from us for liberal purposes. Present conditions demand this.

Let us be clear, abolition is not the revolution itself. However, abolition is a step to bring us closer to revolution, which is a much more extensive process that holds abolition as a method within it. We all know the question that arises from this. Yes, many things will have to be abolished, but what will we replace them with? Before Black people moved from "the prison of slavery to the slavery of prison" as Angela Davis once wrote, debates about abolition raged, debates about the degree of rupture that was needed to secure true Black freedom. Ultimately, slavery was not abolished; emancipation became a point of transition in which slavery was merely reformed.[1]

The era we know as "Reconstruction" when Black people made unprecedented gains in a short period of time serves as a warning to us now. Newly held jobs, elected positions, schools, and opportunities were met with white terror, state-sanctioned and otherwise. The onslaught of the Ku Klux Klan worked its way into the reformed society that would re-enslave Black people under new systems of captivity. Southern states generated massive revenues through the convict-leasing of Black people. What we know as mass incarceration is rooted in this sort of "reform" of slavery, a perfect example of past crimes reproducing themselves in the present.

If we are to examine the emancipation of 1865 as a form of abolition, we need to make an important distinction. The abolitionism we embrace has to be radical and cannot be reformist. It has to require a set of politics that cannot be adapted by oppressors to allow the mere restructuring of violent standards. Those politics must embody a bold *fight*, not passive gratitude for alleged rights bestowed by the same institutions that trampled them previously. The Black radicalism that rejected the industry of slavery and that today rejects the slavery of prison must not be whitewashed from revolu-

[1] Angela Y. Davis, "From the Prison of Slavery to the Slavery of Prison: Frederick Douglass and the Convict Lease System," in *The Angela Y. Davis Reader*, edited by Joy James (Malden, MA: Blackwell, 2008), 74–95.

tionary abolitionism. We are tasked with building a nonelectoral movement that's not rooted in legislative efforts, but, in order for that to be feasible, people have to be presented an alternative with revolutionary potential. If we don't maintain the political rigor of a radical, antistate abolition, we will see it stripped of all meaning. We need "abolition" to retain the bold confrontation of slave revolts and prison uprisings. The anticapitalist thrust of the term cannot be lost either; it's capitalism that aided our enslavement in the first place.

The fact that things look different today doesn't necessarily mean they have truly changed. The lure of symbolic change and economic crumbs can be hard for tired people to resist. Fighting is exhausting, and, after doing it for so long, people often want to at least imagine they've won something.

This fatigue has certainly engulfed me. My writing of this text has been repeatedly interrupted. Things I'd hoped to warn against in it are now unfolding before our eyes. I thought they would take years to come, but they're here already, and abolition has become a mainstream topic overnight. A global pandemic, uprisings, and the desperate need for mutual aid and survival programs are present in a way they were not when I started this book.

Maybe more than ever, I'm writing with a feeling of intense pressure. I've felt some version of it my entire life, but writing through the ravages of COVID-19 make things feel more pressing. Countless people have died in this egregious disaster. It's terrifying. Many of the dead are Black people who were always already existing in extreme crisis. Black deaths throughout this pandemic have been disproportionate to the rest of the population. But that is always the case within this deadly empire, isn't it?

Looking at the work of Sylvia Wynter has helped me process the problems we face. Black people, contrary to liberal myths of progress, are becoming increasingly disposable in U.S. society. Explicitly or through more subtle means, our deaths are dismissed as a form of "natural selection." This term has been used and misdefined in relation to the deaths of Black people to deride our dying as part of an inevitable, inescapable fate. For Darwin, natural selection described how populations adapt, change, and evolve. Wynter gives a particular insight here by addressing what she describes as "Man's overrepresentation." Western culture has long been preoccupied with the idea of "Man." Her work addresses "Man" in two overrepresented forms.[2] One of these forms is "the theocentric conception of the human, Christian, and the new humanist and ratiocentric conception of the human . . . the political subject of the state."[3] The other form is the "Darwinian variant of Man: one in which the

[2] Sylvia Wynter, "Unsettling the Coloniality of Being/Power/Truth/Freedom: Towards the Human, after Man, Its Overrepresentation—an Argument," *CR: The New Centennial Review* 3, no. 3 (2003): 257–337.

[3] Ibid., 269

Human Other malediction or curse, one shared with all the now colonized nonwhite peoples classified as 'natives' (but as their extreme nigger form) would be no longer that of Noah or Nature, but of Evolution and Natural Selection."[4] This "Human Other" is the naturally "dysselected." Wynter's description of the "Darwinian variant of Man" can help us grasp why we see this careless dissemination of "natural selection" as a response to COVID-19 and other crises we have and will encounter. For some, our deaths are certainly fatalistic, a divine circumstance willed by God. However, for others, it's handed down not by any deity but by evolution.

Wynter explains, "This principle, that of bio-evolutionary Natural Selection, was now to function at the level of the new bourgeois social order as a de facto new Argument-from-Design—one in which while one's selected or dysselected status could not be known in advance, it would come to be verified by one's (or one's group's) success or failure in life."[5] For Black people, in ways both obvious and hidden, the deplorable conditions we are subjected to and the many causes of our deaths are seen as preordained in our very biology.

We see our "dysselected" status whenever we look in the mirror.

---

[4] Ibid., 307.
[5] Ibid., 310.

We live in a world of white supremacist apartheid, eugenics, and excess death statistics. In order to move forward at all we have to work toward the end of white supremacy—and whiteness itself. We see the violence of both realized in the state. Black anarchist abolitionism does not stop at prisons, policing, or the military. The entire culture and reality of society in the United States and the white ethnostate project must be fought against, overturned, and reorganized. Whiteness and white supremacy, which do not mean "white people," must be destroyed before they destroy us all.

A Black anarchic abolitionism should work to end the dominion and authority and life of the U.S. state, which bolsters itself through the racist violence it sanctions. Aimé Césaire once wrote:

> One of the values invented by the bourgeoisie in former times and launched throughout the world was *man*—and we have seen what has become of that. The other was the *nation*. It is a fact: the *nation* is a bourgeois phenomenon. Exactly; but if I turn my attention from *man* to *nations*, I note that here too there is great danger; that colonial enterprise is to the modern world what Roman imperialism was to the ancient world: the prelude to Disaster and the forerunner of Catastrophe. Come, now! The Indians massacred, the Moslem world drained of itself, the Chinese world defiled and perverted for a good century; the Negro world disqualified; mighty voices stilled forever; homes scattered to the

Untitled

wind; all this wreckage, all this waste, humanity reduced to a mono-
logue, and you think that all that does not have its price? The truth is
that this policy *cannot but bring about the ruin of Europe itself.*[6]

The ruin of "Europe," of Western rationality, and the white supremacist state is not happening fast enough. We must help it come
faster because history shows us that the state will not simply fade
or wither away. To end white supremacy, we must end the state that
enforces it. I live in the United States, but this conflict is not contained here. The state formation misnamed "America" has been
shaped through whiteness and, as Gerald Horne notes, the "diabol-
ical 'genius' of settler colonialism" in which "those who had once
been victimized by enslavers instead were invited to become enslavers themselves—or perfidious discriminators—in the new guise
of 'whiteness.' "[7]

This helped set North America apart in its political and economic
formation. White people who were once considered lower and
lesser by the ruling class were enlisted as soldiers, scouts, overseers,
and slave catchers. They became "white" and were thus given a rea-

[6] Aimé Césaire, *Discourse on Colonialism* (New York: Monthly Review Press,
1972), 74 (emphasis in original).

[7] Gerald Horne, *The Dawning of the Apocalypse: The Roots of Slavery, White
Supremacy, Settler Colonialism, and Capitalism in the Long Sixteenth Century*
(New York: Monthly Review Press, 2020), 24.

son to feel a species of solidarity with their oppressors. It was whiteness, a social designation that evolved over time, that divorced many of these people from the possibilities, shared experiences, and understandings that saw them joining, on occasion, with Black and Native people in uprisings. White people were granted authority through whiteness by the state, and it is in turn a violent tool used to maintain the white supremacist state. The rebellions that made whiteness necessary in North America were already present in resistance to the "violent social order" of Europe, whose laboring classes provided "the state and its privileged classes with the material and human resources needed for their maintenance and further accumulations of power and wealth."[8] Cedric Robinson uses the term "racial capitalism" to define the historical process that connects feudalism to racism and ultimately to capitalism.[9] Capitalism emerged out of societies and civilization that were racialized, which provided a foundational directive for the structuring of the racist establishments we have to remove from our pathway to liberation now.

The malignancy of whiteness as it took shape in the United States spread throughout the world, growing in virulence and in its ability to wreak havoc. Hitler was famously inspired by the U.S. state. In 1928, he admiringly said the United States had "gunned down the

[8] Cedric J. Robinson, *Black Marxism: The Making of the Black Radical Tradition* (Chapel Hill: University of North Carolina Press, 2000), 21.

[9] Ibid., 2.

millions of Redskins to a few hundred thousand, and now keep the modest remnant under observation in a cage."[10] In *Mein Kampf*, he praised the United States as the "one state" that had worked toward a "better conception" of race-based citizenship.[11] American whiteness was exporting new and vicious forms of segregation, imprisonment, and genocidal violence. Hitler is presented as a historical exception, an aberration, when in reality he is part of a lineage that includes men like King Leopold, Andrew Jackson, and George W. Bush.

Frantz Fanon once recalled Aimé Césaire saying, "When I turn on my radio, when I hear that Negroes have been lynched in America, I say that we have been lied to: Hitler is not dead; when I turn on my radio, when I learn that Jews have been insulted, mistreated, persecuted, I say that we have been lied to: Hitler is not dead; when, finally, I turn on my radio and hear that in Africa forced labor has been inaugurated and legalized, I say that we have certainly been lied to: Hitler is not dead."[12] Césaire also reminds us where Hitler is today. He describes the "distinguished, very humanistic, very Christian bourgeois of the twentieth century": "He has a Hitler in-

[10] James Q. Whitman, *Hitler's American Model: The United States and the Making of Nazi Race Law* (Princeton, NJ: Princeton University Press, 2017), 9.

[11] Ibid., 45.

[12] Fanon, *Black Skin, White Masks*, 66.

side him, that Hitler *inhabits* him, that Hitler is his *demon*."[13] Hitler is very much alive and well in the white supremacists around us. Those politicians, pastors, police, personnel, and others who vehemently defend the white supremacist U.S. state indeed have Hitler, plantation owners, presidents, colonizers, Klansmen, imperialist soldiers, and slavers inside them. Césaire describes the sort of complacency and feigned shock we still see today:

> People are surprised, they become indignant. They say: "How strange! But never mind—it's Nazism, it will pass!" And they wait, and they hope; and they hide the truth from themselves, that it is barbarism, the supreme barbarism, the crowning barbarism that sums up all the daily barbarisms; that it is Nazism, yes, but that before they were its victims, they were its accomplices; that they tolerated that Nazism before it was inflicted on them, that they absolved it, shut their eyes to it, legitimized it, because, until then, it had been applied only to non-European peoples; that they have cultivated that Nazism, that they are responsible for it, and that before engulfing the whole edifice of Western, Christian civilization in its reddened waters, it oozes, seeps, and trickles from every crack.[14]

Black people cannot afford to engage in such nonsense. We need to break through the complacent, liberal veneer that enables and

[13] Césaire, *Discourse on Colonialism*, 36.
[14] Ibid.

strengthens fascism while expressing dismay over the destruction it causes. The distorted legacy of the civil rights movement is part of this subterfuge. The white ethno-state is a fascist dream that cannot be reasoned with.

If bringing about the end of the white supremacist U.S. state does not mean raising up another state in its place, what *does* it mean? One thing it means is that we should seriously investigate the position of the many variations of Black anarchism that insist states are *never* a necessary project. When we revisit Huey P. Newton's concept of intercommunalism, we understand Black nationalism, nation-based sovereignty, and nationhood to be in conflict with the reality of global capitalism. Reflecting on the Black Panther Party, Newton wrote:

> We called ourselves Black Nationalists because we thought that nation-hood was the answer. Shortly after that we decided that what was really needed was revolutionary nationalism, that is, nationalism plus social-ism. After analyzing conditions a little more, we found that it was im-practical and even contradictory. Therefore, we went to a higher level of consciousness. We saw that in order to be free we had to crush the ruling circle and therefore we had to unite with the peoples of the world. So we called ourselves Internationalists. We sought solidarity with the peoples of the world. We sought solidarity with what we thought were the nations of the world. But then what happened? We found that be-cause everything is in a constant state of transformation, because of

the development of technology, because of the development of the mass media, because of the fire power of the imperialist, and because of the fact that the United States is no longer a nation but an empire, nations could not exist, for they did not have the criteria for nationhood. Their self-determination, economic determination, and cultural determination [have] been transformed by the imperialists and the ruling circle. They were no longer nations.... Internationalism, if I understand the word, means the interrelationship among a group of nations. But since no nation exists, and since the United States is in fact an empire, it is impossible for us to be Internationalists. These transformations and phenomena require us to call ourselves "intercommunalists" because nations have been transformed into communities of the world.[15]

Intercommunalism is a useful model of our current world that delegitimizes states and imagines borderless affinities among oppressed peoples, while acknowledging empire and global capitalism. This is not to homogenize or deny the differences of Black people within and beyond the borders of the United States. It is to say simply that we must reject the futile ventures that have mesmerized Black radicals in the past. History is here to teach us, not to be imitated and duplicated without our reevaluation. Intercommunalism

[15] Huey P. Newton, "Speech Delivered at Boston College: November 18, 1970," in *To Die for the People: The Writings of Huey P. Newton*, edited by Toni Morrison (New York: Vintage, 1972), 31–32.

traces a process of internal critique, growth, and understanding that can be beneficial to us today. That development was internalized and taken further by Black anarchism and radical Black autonomy, and we should be willing to take it even further. We have to overcome the lie that nations and states are necessary and that borders and citizenship serve Black people seeking liberation.

The anarcho-syndicalist Rudolf Rocker describes national citizenship as "a political confession of faith." Moreover, he says, it is an oath that happens under the threat of violence. No one has the option to *not* belong to a state, not even those of us who are citizens in name only—or only when it is convenient for our oppressors. Rocker's understanding of the relationship between the nation and the state is also very perceptive.

> The old opinion which ascribes the creation of the nationalist state to the awakened national consciousness of the people is but a fairy tale, very serviceable to the supporters of the idea of the national state, but false, none the less. *The nation is not the cause, but the result, of the state. It is the state which creates the nation, not the nation the state.* Indeed; from this point of view there exists between people and nation the same distinction as between society and the state.... Peoples and groups of peoples existed long before the state put in its appearance. Today, also, they exist and develop without the assistance of the state. ... A people is always a community with rather narrow boundaries. But

a nation, as a rule, encompasses a whole array of different peoples and groups of peoples who have by more or less violent means been pressed into the frame of a common state.[16]

Even in personal interactions, shared identity is not always a sufficient basis for trust, just as we know it isn't in terms of representation in governance. We certainly cannot trust the idea of the nation or the state that facilitates such an idea in the first place. That's not to say that Black nationalism has never accomplished anything. It has. However, technically, so have liberal policy-making and reform. What they have accomplished can still be fleeting and hollow, a simulation of change rather than truly change itself. We need to move beyond strategies that reproduce such results. We've seen reformists take pride in a victory—a new law, new governance—with dwindling attention to how, or whether, it has fundamentally changed people's lives. After all, it is the people who make revolutions happen, even though leaders, politicians, and bureaucrats get all the credit. It has happened all across the world, and there are plenty of examples to draw from. Regarding nationalist causes, we are obliged to take into consideration independence struggles on the African continent and throughout the African diaspora. We cannot simply idealize or ignore what happened in places like Guyana,

[16] Rudolf Rocker, *Nationalism and Culture* (Montreal: Black Rose Books, 1998), 200–201 (emphasis in original).

The view from the Edmund Pettus Bridge

Ethiopia, Ghana, Guinea, and elsewhere in the name of revolutionary nationalism and nation-building.

Elder activist and former statesman Eusi Kwayana experienced these problems firsthand in Guyana. He wrote, "Experience in the newly independent countries teaches us that a national bourgeoisie can arise in various ways." Of the political elite, he observed, "The new rulers . . . except for their public positions and political slogans, are carbon copies of the old colonial officials. They differ verbally, but not inwardly."[17] Kwayana's younger contemporary Walter Rodney also noted, "The dominant mode of thinking in Africa today is inherited from the colonial masters and is given currency by the state apparatus." Rodney added, "The unity of Africa requires the unity of progressive groups, organizations and institutions rather than merely being the preserve of states."[18] It's about *us* and what *we* do, not the fictional narrative that we require authority and leadership as Black people. Masses of people working together are more important than trying to reproduce the exhausted, reformist goal of seizing state power to move our struggles closer to liberation.

[17] Eusi Kwayana, *The Bauxite Strike and the Old Politics* (Atlanta: On Our Own Authority!, 2014), 85, 86.

[18] Walter Rodney, "Aspects of the International Class Struggle in Africa, the Caribbean and America," in *Pan-Africanism: Struggle against Neo-Colonialism and Imperialism—Documents of the Sixth Pan-African Congress*, edited by Horace Campbell (Toronto: Afro-Carib Publications, 1975), 18–41.

At the same time, regardless of the internal power grabs and the reinstitution of class structures and inequalities, we also cannot ignore what imperial forces did, and always will do, to stop all liberatory efforts. We need to examine victories, failures, and atrocities, from within and without, in order to direct our path, not to simply follow those already trodden. This nation on no map, Black America, can turn away from the false promises of recognition through nationhood or citizenship and surpass the state. We can find our revolutionary collective liberation beyond flags, banners, and parties. After all, some of us are descended from the enslaved because of the betrayals of nations, one group of people pitting themselves against another for dominance, aligning themselves with powerful invaders for political and economic benefit. Our past is a cautionary tale, a lesson for us today as we try to shape a future that avoids repeating past mistakes.

Simply detaching ourselves from the state is not enough. We're charged with growing our own survival programs, institutions, and survival economies as a means of building a revolutionary movement that can effectively challenge the state. We'll have to be able to present masses of people with revolutionary options that can actually meet day-to-day needs like food, housing, and health care. We should remind each other through support and love what "The Anarchism of Blackness" tried to illustrate: Black people throughout the world have already long practiced anarchic principles and created anarchic projects out of necessity. Our "assertions of Black personhood, humanity and liberation have necessarily called into question both the foundations and legitimacy of the American state."[19] Our experiences already, to quote Mbah and Igariwey, affirm and "lend credence to the historical truism that governments have not always existed. They are but a recent phenomenon and are, therefore, not inevitable in human society."[20] This much is true for Black people throughout the African diaspora and all across the African continent. Indigenous anarchists have long explained that the practices ascribed to anarchist ideology precede nineteenth-century origins of "anarchism" as a named social movement and indeed precede the nation-state itself. However, as Indigenous anarchism, autonomous movements, and stateless people everywhere can surely attest, we cannot simply turn our back on the state and hope it goes away; nor can we seek new, or even old, ways of living outside the state and assume it will ignore us.

If we are honest, we know we must seek the total destruction of the oppressive forces that limit our capacity to survive. Survival work is not something we do to coexist with oppressive forces and, even less, to reform the state by example. It must be done to sustain

[19] William C. Anderson and Zoé Samudzi, "The Anarchism of Blackness," *ROAR Magazine* 5 (Spring 2017): 77.

[20] Sam Mbah and I. E. Igariwey, *African Anarchism: The History of a Movement* (Victoria, BC: Camas Books, 2018), 27.

ourselves *as* we work to dismantle and take down the apparatuses of power. Without clear revolutionary content, mutual aid, survival programs, and even horizontalist organizing can be co-opted and absorbed into the state's infrastructure. We must be unabsorbable, or as Lorenzo Kom'boa Ervin once told me, we "have to make ourselves and our communities ungovernable."[21] This is not about charity or philanthropy; it's about solidarity in the face of state violence, and sustenance that can help propel us forward to confront the purveyors of that violence. State-building and militant posturing are only so much political cosplay: they neglect the work that must be done on the ground and among the people, among ourselves, to abolish the historical structures and logics that have brought us to this point. As Ashanti Alston has said: "To be a revolutionary requires a certain daringness, a certain sense of Harriet Tubman that goes in and out from North to South to keep freeing people. [And] you have to be willing to take a risk that might take your life, but it's going to free somebody."[22] This pursuit isn't all about endings. It's also about new beginnings.

Speaking on the Du Boisian notion of abolition democracy and

[21] William C. Anderson, "Ungovernable: An Interview with Lorenzo Kom'boa Ervin," Black Rose Anarchist Federation blog, September 11, 2020, blackrosefed .org/ungovernable-interview-lorenzo-komboa-ervin-anderson.

[22] "Ashanti Alston," *Treyf Podcast*, interview 47, July 28, 2020, www.treyf podcast.com/2020/07/28/47-ashanti-alston.

Reconstruction, Angela Davis remarks: "It is not only, or not even primarily, about abolition as a negative process of tearing down, but it is also about building up, about creating new institutions.... DuBois pointed out that in order to fully abolish the oppressive conditions produced by slavery, new democratic institutions would have to be created. Because this did not occur; black people encountered new forms of slavery—from debt peonage and the convict lease system to segregated and second-class education."[23]

A lesson here is that abolishing or readjusting one aspect of the systematic state violence we face is never enough; it allows oppressive structures and violence room to expand and become more effective in other areas. Formal state-bestowed (and thus within the state's logic) voting rights meant very little in the face of a thousand other oppressions great and small. Repeatedly telling ourselves that the violence of colonialism and white supremacy will somehow be defeated by the same reasoning and methodology they employ is clearly a self-defeating strategy. If we can see the dangers in state-building or the bourgeois values of the nation as Césaire described, we must acknowledge the failures of many projects we'd call our own. It means admitting the hard truth of what is not the path to freedom.

[23] Angela Y. Davis, *Abolition Democracy: Beyond Empire, Prisons, and Torture* (New York: Seven Stories Press, 2005), 69.

Reflecting on her experiences in Guyana, Sylvia Wynter challenges us to go further:

> What I had witnessed there—the failure of [the] Marxist project in Guyana in bringing about the transformation which would cut across the Black/Indian divide—gave me much to think about concerning our problems. Yes, we had supported the Marxists, and we realized very quickly that the state solution given by the Marxists was not sufficient because of the prevalence of race, that the work needs to occur elsewhere, aside from the state. . . . We were able to forego that cheap and easy radicalism of simply organizing the state differently and we began to tell different origin stories of who we were as Blacks and as Africans. It was the creative side and the creative working of things which led us to the difference in making claims about who we are. The cheap and easy radicalism does not address the underlying requirement for a total transformation—who are we as Black people, as Africans? The Marxists, and actually no party could give us that. Only we could do it! That is the easy way. The hard way is to reclaim our past, present and future selves, totally![24]

In a similar vein, Marx writes, "The social revolution of the nine-

[24] Bedour Alagraa, "What Will Be the Cure? A Conversation with Sylvia Wynter," *Offshoot Journal*, January 7, 2021, offshootjournal.org/what-will-be-the-cure-a-conversation-with-sylvia-wynter.

teenth century cannot take its poetry from the past but only from the future. It cannot begin with itself before it has stripped off all superstition in regard to the past. Earlier revolutions required recollections of past world history in order to drug themselves concerning their own content. In order to arrive at its own content, the revolution of the nineteenth century must let the dead bury their dead. There the phrase went beyond the content; here the content goes beyond the phrase."[25]

The failure of the "cheap and easy" radicalism Sylvia Wynter speaks of shows us that the state is not the answer to our problems. The state cannot solve problems that it cannot comprehend, because it is a weapon that was not designed to rectify them. Furthermore, many of our problems predate it and will likely follow after its dissolution. If our activity doesn't bring us closer to total transformation but merely advocates partial or piecemeal changes arbitrated by the state, we're sabotaging our struggle. Obviously, revolutionary change rarely, if ever, comes all at once. Nonetheless, it is important that we keep a complete picture in the forefront of our minds, so that we can see the complexity of everything around us.

Black anarchism can answer *some* of the questions we need to ask in order to transcend the present state of things, a world of colonial-

[25] Karl Marx, *The Eighteenth Brumaire of Louis Bonaparte* (New York: International Publishers, 1963), 18.

ism, slavery, exploitation, and hierarchy. I have found Black anarchism useful because it doesn't focus on just one aspect of the problem. It looks at the whole of history and works to uproot oppression by asking the most basic questions about what power is and what gives anyone the right to control or oppress others, even those we share space with. The question is simple, but its implications are vast, influencing the totality of our lives from race to gender to class and all of the many aspects of existence into which power insinuates itself.

No ideology, however, has all the answers. Just as Black anarchism should be critical of authoritarianism, elitism, and religiosity, it must also be critical of itself. We must analyze and expose the blatant contradictions we see in the white supremacist state, as well as among the zealous proponents of any ideology, including various Black anarchisms. That's why for me, Black anarchism is not just antistate, it can embody the anti-ideology and anti-cultism force needed to create new outlooks. In turn, we should be working to exceed our very selves. We're trying to figure this out as we go, but it can be said without a doubt that nothing is going to change if people keep attempting to reinvent radical traditions. The beauty of what worked before becomes ugly through the staleness of repetition.

Understanding the need to confront the white supremacist state and understand our position as Black people within its confines does not mean we seek out nationality or nationhood. We don't need to know our exact ancestral origins to know we're Africans. We don't have to centralize anything or homogenize ourselves to confront the tragedy that we know as the United States. Be wary of any one-size-fits all rhetoric that glosses over the unfathomable diversity of Black people. Absolutist approaches destroy possibility. Europe drew the map of the world as we know it—a ranked array of nation-states—using the tools of white supremacy and capitalism. We don't have to use nationhood or nationalism to try to find ourselves on their map. The map, the nation, and the state must go. We did not draw them, and they do not serve us. They never did. To exist on their map in any way can only diminish us and undermine everything that we're capable of.

The U.S. state isn't killing us simply because it's white supremacist: killing is part of the power granted to states, it's what states do. It's what they are built for. It's what their police do, what their militaries do, what their borders do, and what their political parties do. All these things are structured according to the ideas of hierarchical organization and leadership and governance. There is a deadly potential buried in all of them that we must reject. To try to make use of them for "revolutionary" purposes means running toward goals that have nothing to do with true liberation. We must not remain trapped on this map; we must try to draw new lines to sketch out a life for ourselves that their borders, their states, and their map cannot hold.

Our task is to shape a new society, a world we want to live in. In order to do so, we have to do away with the old one. The state will never end state violence, nor will any politics that relies on it.

"Anarchism" is just a name. Our revolution can be great no matter what we call it, and we shouldn't use the words "revolution" or "revolutionaries" lightly. Lucy Parsons gives instruction: "When you roll under your tongue the expression that you are revolutionists, remember what that word means. It means a revolution that shall turn all these things over where they belong."[26] There is a lot to overthrow and to sabotage and to leave in utter ruination. We can draw new horizons with the pen of self-determination, but first we must do some erasing. We must be ungovernable masses to create a society where safety and abundance rule over us, not violence.

There's no avoiding it, the fight that's all around us. This is a time that requires us to choose freedom from all oppressive formations. The new, liberated future we hope to grasp comes closer to us through the willingness to first hold the truth of where we are now and where we have already been.

---

[26] Lucy Parsons, "Speeches at the Founding Convention of the Industrial Workers of the World," in *Freedom, Equality and Solidarity—Writings and Speeches, 1878–1937* (Chicago: Charles H. Kerr, 2004), 81.

A LETTER TO THE READER

Developing a new anticapitalist ideology or radical critique is never easy, but it's necessary if we are to truly move forward and obtain the freedom of Black people. In *The Nation on No Map*, William C. Anderson has bravely stepped forward and offered his views in the face of criticism, ideological posturing, and even personal hatred, typical of political dialogue in this period.

William is breaking new ground, making radical critiques of both Black and anarchist theory. He rejects the ideal of left-liberal civil rights activism, which he believes just preserves the state and legalism. He sees these as social control rather than true liberation. He rejects Black citizenship, which is limited to chauvinism, representative democracy, and reformism. He calls this a complete fraud and only halfway measures, since America was founded as a white racist republic and the American Revolution was a white slave master rebellion against the English Crown.

William denounces bogus royal lineage that claims all Black people enslaved in the "new world" are descended from kings and queens. Royals were often parasites and oppressors themselves, and this scam totally denies that there was class oppression in ancient African cultures.

William says we need to understand that Black royalty, fame, and celebrity are means of social control and false social capital to make us think we are engaging in progress. He is trying to tell us that this is as much of a farce as Wakanda or the African king played by Eddie Murphy.

Some of William's sharpest criticism is reserved for the leftist and authoritarian movements betraying their entire history and ideology by crushing workers, the poor, peasants, and other people due to outright dictatorships and mass murderers as heads of the state.

William doesn't look to Black nationalism or any form of Black statism to take us forward to freedom.

Black anarchism, with its rejection of radical political orthodoxy, a place where I started my own political critique in the 1970s, is the place where William has also arrived. He realizes, just as I did, that the state must be abolished, not reformed, along with the entire capitalist system.

Such a Black critique can serve as political education for all anarchists, to light their way through the contemporary radical ideology and to denounce the dead politics and theories of yesteryear. Even anarchism, grounded in so much white radicalism, needs to be rewritten and reinterpreted by Black anarchist activist writers. Its perspective needs to be sharpened.

When I wrote *Anarchism and the Black Revolution* in 1979, it was the first time a Black anarchist raised the theories and perspective of colonized and oppressed Blacks in the United States. It no doubt embarrassed many anarchists but energized many more toward antiracism and decolonization. Daring to challenge the conventional wisdom earns enemies and friends, yet activist writers have to be honest and not spare feelings when that time comes. William C. Anderson has done that in *The Nation on No Map*.

Black anarchism, in whatever form, is here to stay. A new wave has come just in the last five years. Some Black anarchists differ from me, though for sure we are not enemies. These new Black anarchists do not have a unitary belief system, but they have the right to self-awareness and their own ideological leanings, which are decidedly non-European.

Nobody can tell them they don't belong, just as they could not tell me that I didn't belong over the last forty-eight years. We are here, and we ain't going nowhere! We will continue to innovate, critique, organize, and write about the ideals of radical anarchism.

This is what you're hearing from William C. Anderson, one of the best young Black anarchist writers and thinkers. You better appreciate him!

LORENZO KOM'BOA ERVIN

INDEX

Black history: and capitalist historians, 69–70; critiquing past movements, 66–7; ethics in research, 76; historical distortions, 6, 101, 103; and nationalist pride, 14; prioritizing mythology (*see* royalty); violence as needed, 101. *See also various Black history events*

Black Liberation Army, 112, 137

Black nationalism: accomplishments, 174; ADOS, 147–8; Black Panther Party, 148–9, 171–2; Garvey and UNIA, 145–6, 154; and innocence myth, 155; Liberia, 153–4; and masses, 156; Nation of Islam, 149–52; and white supremacists, 146, 152, 153

Black Panther Party for Self Defense: overview, 27–8; and communism, 88–9; hating oppressors, 65; ideology of, 171–2; limitations of, 81–2; nationalism, 148–9, 171–2; NBPP, 148–9; survival programs, 28, 30–2, 36. *See also* Newton, Huey P.

Black Power, 81–2, 101, 103

Black Reconstruction (Du Bois), 26–7, 75–6, 98

Black Wall Street, 128, 142

Blackness, 23–4, 27, 113

"Blackstone Rangers" (Brooks), xxvii

Bloody Sunday commemoration, 7

Bodhidharma, 84–5

bombings, 129, 131

book overview, xiii–xvii, xxvi–xxix, 187–9

Brand, Dionne, 3, 106–7

Brooks, Gwendolyn, xxvii

Browne, Simone, 127

Buddhism, 84–5, 87

capitalism: Black people's relationship to, 39, 53–5, 57–60, 65; and exploitation, 52; Garvey and UNIA, 154; and oppression, 39–40; racial capitalism, 168; and the state, 77–8. *See also* wealth

celebrity/fame, 51, 57–8, 59–64, 69, 74–5. *See also* royalty

centralism, 88–90

Césaire, Aimé, xxii, 44, 165, 167, 169–70

change, 157, 171–2

citizenship: vs. begging, 119; as invention, 21; and Obama, 23; Robeson, 64–5; threats of

East Germany, 20
ecological emergencies, 115–6
Egypt, 42
elections, 9–11, 13–4, 22, 28. *See also* political parties
elitism, 84
emancipation, 26–7, 121, 160–1
Emancipation Proclamation, 26
England, 18–9
Ervin, JoNina, xxv
Ervin, Lorenzo Kom'boa: and Anderson, xxv; on Anderson and book, 187–9; on building autonomy, 117; on civil rights movement, 8; on communes, 109; on communism, 79–80; and Cuba, 19; disillusioned with Black leaders, 59; as former military, 137; on intercommunalism and anarchism, 32; on NBPP, 149; and Sostre, 20, 151; on task of revolutionaries, 138; on ungovernability, 179; on vanguardism, 80–1
European anarchism. *See also* anarchism; classical anarchism
Every Cook Can Govern (James), 116

Facing Reality (James), 77–8
failure, 180

Fanon, Frantz, 50, 139–40, 141, 156
fascism: Black people knowing, 35; and communism, 80; Ice Cube and ADOS, 149; and innocence, 155; and liberalism, 170–1; Nation of Islam, 150–1; UNIA as, 145–6
fatigue, 162
fighting. *See* state of war
"Framing the Panther" (James), 28, 30
freedom, defined, 25–6, 27

gangs, 135–7
Garvey, Marcus, 145–6, 154
genealogy industry, 46, 48–50
gentrification, 97, 105, 106, 115
Georgia, 132–3
Gilroy, Paul, 145–6, 149, 155
"Giving Up Patriotism and Integration Myths for MLK Day" (Anderson), 14–5
Global South, 103–4
Gloria Richardson, 119
goals, 62, 94
Goode, W. Wilson, Sr., 131
Gramsci, Antonio, 76–7
The Great Migration, 96–7, 99. *See also* migration
Guyana, 176, 181

90–1; civil rights movement, 6, 8; in classical anarchism, 83, 85–7; fetishization, 86–7; Garvey as, 146; Malcolm X as, 55; in state of war, 136; and subjectivism, 88–90; and wealth, 53–5

the left: charging counterrevolution, 90; defined, 68; as dogmatic, 71–4, 75, 82, 90, 93–4; and history of movements, 66–7; leaders and authoritarian left, 73, 78, 86–7, 90–1; mythologies, 68–71, 73–5, 87–8; the state becoming the people, 77–9; vangaurdism, 80–1. *See also* anarchism

legislation vs. social revolution, 8. *See also* reform

Lenin, Vladimir, 88–9

LGBTQ+, 134, 137, 151

liberalism, 15. *See also* reform

liberation: and accumulation, 40; and boundaries, 1; as collective, 62; and land, 107, 115–6; vs. reformism, 93–4 (*see also* reform); vs. relative improvements, 27; struggle to experience, 25–7; superstitions, 1–2

Liberia, 153–4

Lin-Chi, 87

Lorde, Audre, xxix–xxx

Los Angeles, 98

Lost Cause, 123

loyalties, 67

Lutalo, Ojore, 82

Malcolm X, 54, 55, 106, 152, 159

Man, 163–4, 165, 167

management of Black people, 53–5. *See also* leaders

martyrdom, 15, 73, 83

Marx, Karl, 71–2, 74, 181–2

Marxism, xxii, 79–80, 82, 181. *See also* communism

the masses/the people: anarchism and, 91–2; Fanon on, 156; and power of leaders, 71, 89; and revolution, 174; as ungovernable, xvi, 185

Mbah, Sam, 178

media, 53

Mexico, 16, 18

middle class, 15

migration: overview, 95–8; across the world, 99–100; community networks, 114–5; as constant, 100; and gentrification, 97, 105, 106; from Global South, 103, 104–5; in state of war, 140 military, 137

MOVE, 129, 131

mutual aid, 35–6

mythologies, 68–70, 73–6, 87–8. *See also* royalty

Nation of Islam (NOI), 149–52

nation on no map, xxvii–xxviii, 100–1, 177, 184–5. *See also* Black citizenship; statelessness

nationalism, 14, 125, 156, 184. *See also* Black nationalism

nations: Césaire on, 165, 167; and natural resources, 20–1; rights documents vs. reality, 21, 23; and Robeson, 64–5; and the state, 173–4. *See also* Black citizenship; citizenship; statelessness

Native Americans, 49, 168–9. *See also* Indigenous Peoples

natural resources, 20–1

natural selection, 163–4

Nazism, 77, 78, 80, 168–70

Nelson, Alondra, 48–50

New Black Panther Party (NBPP), 148–9

Newton, Huey P., 28, 31–2, 33, 108–9, 171–2

Nixon, Richard, 59

No Selves to Defend (Kaba), 134

North vs. South in America, 105–6

Obama, Barack, 23

Otherness, 163–4

outrage, 142–3

Pan Africanism, 32

Parsons, Lucy, 11, 13, 185

patriarchy, xxix–xxx

patriotism, 6

perpetual reactivity, 83–4

"The 'Pet Negro' System" (Hurston), 106

philanthropy, 40–1

police, 132–3, 143

political parties, 33, 51, 68. *See also* voting

poor people, 15

Portugal, 18

poverty pimps, 58

power, 42, 88–90

preemptive planning, 35–6

prisons, 26, 36–8, 160–1

race, 48–9

race war, 124. *See also* white supremacy

racial capitalism, 168

sexism, xxix–xxx
Shakur, Assata, 30, 39
sharecropping, 26
Sharpe, Christina, 99
Shelby County v. Holder, 9–10
slavery: Africans participation in,
   45–6, 177; and displacement, 98;
   documentation of, 147–8; emancipation, 26–7, 121, 160–1; police
   during, 132–3; prisons as continua-
   tion of, 26; reformed, 161; reparations, 147–8, 149; and Scotts'
   court battle, 15–6; surveillance,
   127
socialism, 71–2. *See also* communism
soldiers, 125–6
Sostre, Martin, 20, 82, 119, 137, 151
the South, 105–6, 120–3
Soviet Union, 87–8
Spillers, Hortense, 44
squatters, 110
Stalin, Joseph, 77, 78, 80
the state: overview, xiv–xv, 125 (*see
   also* reform); Black Panther's survival programs, 28, 30–2, 36; and
   capitalism, 77–8; dogma of, 86;
   during ecological emergencies,
   115–6; Marxism in Guyana, 181;
   and nations, 173–4; power to kill,

184; rectifying problems, 182;
   reproducing exclusion, 107–8;
   revolutionaries and myths, 75;
   and ruling elites history, 77; sacrifice for, 101; threat from, 93; as
   white supremacist, 122. *See also*
   communism
state building, 142, 143, 145–7, 153–4.
   See also Black nationalism
*State Capitalism and World Revolu-
   tion* (James, Dunayevskaya, and
   Boggs), 77
state of war: overview, 119–20; allies,
   136; Birmingham, AL, 129; and
   citizenship, 125–6; Detroit 1967,
   129; discussions of defense, 124;
   emancipation, 121; and fatigue,
   162; and leaders, 136; MOVE, 129,
   131; police, 132–3; police brutality
   uprisings, 132; romanticizing, 120;
   self-defense, 135–9, 143; in the
   South, 120–4; and state building,
   142, 143, 145–7, 157 (*see also* Black
   nationalism); and statelessness,
   125–6, 140–1; surveillance, 126–8;
   Tulsa, OK, 128; women and girls,
   134–5
statelessness: as all encompassing,
   125; Ervin, 19–20; and migration,

ited, 52; and liberation myth, 39–40; trickle down, 40–1; and value, 42. *See also* capitalism

white supremacy: and capitalism, 53–4; and citizenship, 119; and destruction of communities, 142; extremism, 122; and Garvey, 146; and The Great Migration, 99; Hitler inhabiting, 170; race war, 124; reactionary responses to, 145; and Reconstruction, 98–9; rejection of, 25; in the South, 121–4; Tulsa, OK, 128; and white people, 165; and whiteness, 167–8. *See also* state of war

whiteness, 82, 167–8

Williams, Robert F., 19–20

Windrush generation, 18–9

women, 28, 30, 134, 136

working class, 15, 52

Wynter, Sylvia, 163–4, 181

Yarbrough, Camille, 55, 57–9, 143

Yüan (Master), 85–6

Zen Buddhism, 84–5, 87

FRIENDS OF AK PRESS

AK Press is small, in terms of staff and resources, but we also manage to be one of the world's most productive anarchist publishing houses. We publish close to twenty books every year, and distribute thousands of other titles published by like-minded independent presses and projects from around the globe. We're entirely worker run and democratically managed. We operate without a corporate structure—no boss, no managers, no bullshit.

The Friends of AK program is a way you can directly contribute to the continued existence of AK Press, and ensure that we're able to keep publishing books like this one! Friends pay $25 a month directly into our publishing account ($30 for Canada, $35 for international), and receive a copy of every book AK Press publishes for the duration of their membership! Friends also receive a discount on anything they order from our website or buy at a table: 50 percent on AK titles, and 30 percent on everything else. We have a Friends of AK e-book program as well: $15 a month gets you an electronic copy of every book we publish for the duration of your membership. You can even sponsor a deeply discounted membership for someone in prison.

Email friendsofak@akpress.org for more info, or visit the website: akpress.org/friends.html.

There are always great book projects in the works—so sign up now to become a Friend of AK Press, and let the presses roll!